The Fire *Still* Burns!

Exploring Church Bullying and Spiritual Abuse

The Fire *Still* Burns!

Exploring Church Bullying and Spiritual Abuse

J. E. Hazlett Lynch

Geneva Christian Publishing

2023

TO

ALL MINISTERS AND SERVANTS OF THE
GOSPEL WHO HAVE EXPERIENCED BULLYING
AND SPIRITUAL ABUSE AT THE HANDS OF
THEIR CHURCHES

You can contact Geneva Christian Publishing at:

West Lynn
23 Parkmore Close
MAGHERAFELT
Co. Londonderry
Northern Ireland
BT45 6PL

x

About the Author

Rev. J. E. Hazlett Lynch, Ph.D, D.Min, was ordained to the Christian ministry in 1979 and worked in several congregations within the Presbyterian Church in Ireland. His preaching was always expository and evangelistic, and sought to explain what the text meant and how its message applied to the present day. In his last charge, he saw twelve people profess faith in Christ within a twenty-one month period. God was obviously blessing his ministry, a fact that the devil and his servants certainly did not appreciate!

Ministering in the dangerous areas of Northern Ireland was one thing, but Dr Lynch found that the outside world was not the only source of 'terrorism.' The church was more than capable of unleashing the deepest pain on Christ's servants by using bullying and spiritual abuse as management tools to keep control of ministers/elders. Dr Lynch was eventually 'loosed from his charge' in 1993, and within fifteen months, had a serious breakdown in his health. This necessitated a long eighteen months under psychiatric care, during which time his psychiatrist was on the verge of sectioning him under the Mental Health Act for his own safety.

These were horrendous times for his whole family. The church put the family out of their home effectively and they had to look for somewhere to live. During that transitionary period of four months, an elder stalked them, causing great unsettlement to his wife, Margaret. These were traumatic times for the family.

Thankfully, they were given the grace to hand this entire unwholesome affair over to God, assured that *'vengeance is Mine; I will repay, says the LORD.'*

Dr Lynch has been married to Margaret since 1973, and they have two sons, David and Stephen. Stephen is married to Julie and they have two lovely children, Mollie and Joshua.

Other books by J. E. Hazlett Lynch

Geneva Christian Publishing published the following books*:*

Seek My Face (2022)

Remembering the Doctor (2021)

Your Refuge in Difficult Times (2020)

God's Greatest Gift (2020)

The Five Books of Moses (2020)

The Seventeen OT Books of History and Wisdom (2020)

The Seventeen Books of the Prophets (2020)

GENEVA – John Calvin's City (2020)

The Tornado of the Pulpit (2018)

To Tell the Truth (2018)

Courage under the Cross (2018)

God's Amazing Love – in preparation. Ambassador Publishing

Lamb of God – Saviour of the World – WestBow Press (2015)

Overcoming Bullying at School – Victim Care Publications (2001)

On the Road to Recovery – Victim Care Publications (1999)

Acknowledgements

I wish to make the following acknowledgements: for time spent with those ministers in various denominations, but mostly with PCI ministers, for the generous amount of time they gave to me and for the support I received from them by simply being with them.

May the Lord be with all His broken and crushed servants, and show them His marvellous grace and mercy, especially when the denominations have refused to administer natural justice, let alone biblical justice, to them.

May He also be with those stressed out wives who have had to live with seriously traumatised husbands for many years, and without any help from the church!

May the manse children also know God's amazing grace as they struggle with what the church has done to their father!

May He be with those church members, and there are many, whom the church has treated abysmally!

I acknowledge all these children of God to be my spiritual siblings. We suffer together. When one member of the Body of Christ suffers, all suffer.

Preface

The fire *still* burns! Why write a book on this subject as it relates to what goes on within Christian denominations?   I had no plans to write on this subject.   These chapters started their life as a series of sermons preached in 2022, and I aimed them at church members; they were not academic lectures but essentially pastoral messages to help Christians gain an understanding of an evil that is bedevilling many evangelical churches and ministers.   It is the 'elephant in the room' about which decent church society does not talk!   While these are not mere academic articles, I trust the following chapters are mindful of the best learning that is available.

My preference, instead, was to write on other biblical issues, expositions of Scripture, and dealing with theological matters.   But, write a book on *Bullying and Spiritual Abuse* within evangelical churches? No way!

William Cowper (1731-1800) is correct when he writes, *'God moves in a mysterious way His wonders to perform.'* Given the growing number of bullying cases within the churches, I felt that I had to address this issue, if for no other reason than this: bullying is essentially an isolating behaviour, and its targets come to believe that only they have ever experienced this wicked behaviour. So they remain silent about what was done to them!

This book is not about ministers bullying their people, though this happens on occasions. Nor is it about the people bullying their ministers! That also happens. It directs attention to the spiritual abuse that ministers inflict on their colleagues in the main, by fellow elders, though not exclusively. The book reveals situations that are horrendous, deception, lies, corruption, high-handedness, scheming and planning behind backs, and so on. Having experienced this horrendous treatment and having researched it for my Master's degree, reliving these awful experiences was not easy. It took its toll on me. Truly, **the fire *still* burns!**

Working through this painful matter, I wondered how the church ever accepted such predators into the Christian ministry! I suppose they concealed who and what they really were to get in!

That raised the question as to what qualities the church was looking for in candidates for the ministry. Was the teaching of Scripture ever seriously consulted as to the qualifications for the eldership? As I recall, the denomination considered only two things during my candidacy: was I a communicant member of a Presbyterian congregation, and was I working towards, or did I have, a university degree! There was no concern shown as to whether or not I was a converted man, or whether I believed the Gospel! Had I a track record of service in the church, or was I looking for a nice, easy, well-paid, job with security of work? The interviewing panel did not explore such matters. In fact, the denomination's Board of Studies presented the Christian ministry to me as a 'career.' I nearly threw-up at the very thought. To me, the ministry was a divine calling unlike any other sphere of work!

On the eldership aspect, I cannot recall the biblical qualifications for this the highest of church offices ever being raised. Looking back now, that was astonishing! That being the case, it is now no shock to see that men of what is essentially 'gangster' mentality are in the Christian ministry! These 'firm's men' seem to be devoid of any scruples when they are on a mission to defend the establishment. Their intent to 'defend the indefensible' is characteristic of them, regardless of who is hurt or destroyed as a result.

A problem with the idea of denominationalism is that once you are in, it expects you to be a good 'firm's man' at all times. Those who prove to be such are 'promoted' (whatever that means within biblical Presbyterianism!) to levels of responsibility and *power* where their rite runs! It is men in such positions who behave as *'Lord's over God's estate'* (1 *Peter* 5:3, Revised Geneva Translation, 21st Century), ignoring the fact that ministers are members of the flock, too. The view seems to be that if ministers in high position do or say a thing, it must be right! Because they hold a 'holy office' within the church (elder), it must mean that all they do and say is also 'holy.' That means they are above any criticism, no matter how legitimate and justified it is! Such confusion is troublesome within the church of Jesus Christ.

Because church leaders are the main perpetrators of *bullying and spiritual abuse*, they are *not* the best-placed people to identify and deal with this ongoing menace. They are too closely associated with 'the establishment.' How true it is that those who benefit from an institution will never seek to change it!

I remember speaking in the summer of 2021 to a senior minister within the church and asking him what steps his church was taking to teach about *bullying and spiritual abuse*. His reply was as brief and it was revealing – *it is not a problem*. The reticence to admit that bullying is going on within the churches is disappointing and serves only to guarantee its continuation, and inflicts a horrendous cost on all involved, perpetrators as well as victims.

Further, one would never expect such wicked behaviour to go on in the Christian church! It is *the* caring profession *par excellence*, and the ministers and elders are the *carers*! They would never stoop to such a level, would they? Their calling is to care for and protect their members and fellow-elders from harm and danger. When the church fails here, she ought not to be surprised that those she damaged are critical of her, and distrustful of anything she says or does. Just look at the growing number of professing Christians who no longer attach themselves to *any* church denomination, or even attend public worship! In any case, you might say, the Bible has nothing to say about *bullying and spiritual abuse*! It is silent!

Not so quick. When the Bible promotes a certain thing, by implication, it condemns the opposite. This was the method used by the Westminster divines when they composed its Catechisms. In explaining the Ten Commandments, they brought out not only what God requires for their observance, but also what He forbids if the commandments were to be observed.

I found this a most helpful approach when dealing with this emotionally charged subject. When Scripture commands us to *'love one another,'* and to *'love your neighbour as yourself,'* it was abundantly clear to me that it is wrong for anyone to contravene this basis principle, be it in church or state!

Bullying is a life-dominating and life-threatening behaviour engaged in by those who target us for *spiritual abuse*. The fact that bullies target other people means that bullying does not happen to us by chance. *'Bullying and spiritual abuse'* is never a random act! Wicked behaviour guarantees a never-to-be-forgotten experience for its victims. Fifteen years after being put through this agony in and by the church, I was faced with a re-run at work when a female committee member abused what power she thought she had to humiliate me. I left work that day, went straight to my GP, and she put me off work for four weeks. I recognised the dynamics that were at work in that situation, and took immediate action. Truly, **the fire *still* burns!**

The experience of bullying is something that never leaves you. You become most vigilant and even the least signs of a recurrence of spiritual abuse are recognised immediately. Indeed, when I hear that the church has done this to others, I am ready for action on their behalf.

Having trained and qualified as a further and higher education college lecturer, I completed my education with a Master's research dissertation, on the subject of *workplace bullying*. Having gained an understanding of what it was that the church did to us, my wife and I promised that if we ever heard of other ministers being put through this horrendous experience, we would be there to support them, if they wanted it. For the past thirty years, we have been providing some support to those unfortunate servants of Christ whose ministries brought them to the notice of their theologically liberal overseers in the church! This also happened to ministers in those churches that would claim to be 'pure'!

Since this is not the place to go into specific details of my case, I will confine my remarks to the limitations set down by the texts that I seek to expound.

CONTENTS

1. Bullying and Spiritual Abuse - An Introduction
John 13:31-37

I am going to address with you a massive elephant that is in the room of every Christian denomination. No one sees it simply because he or she does not want to see it. It is a banned topic of conversation in most churches. Nobody will own up to it; and that is because it *is* there. *They* know it is there. *We* know it is there. However, no one wants to see it. It is the 'Emperor's new clothes' syndrome all over again!

This syndrome has gripped the minds of many of God's people though they will not admit it. Victims have told the church authorities about it repeatedly, but no one wants to open his or her eyes to see it. Moreover, the point is, it is so big you cannot miss it!

Why do I say that? Because once they see it, they have to deal with it. Once they identify the elephant in the room, then they have to take steps to remove it. This is a potentially dangerous elephant, and one that can cause great damage to God's people, and therefore to God's church. Not a few chosen servants willingly engage with this elephant, and that makes the situation worse.

1

That means that the church must ask an outside body

to investigate the situation carefully and independently. It is not acceptable to appoint the friends and colleagues of the bullies to investigate this bullying and spiritually abusive behaviour by their colleagues because such a move would rob any findings of integrity. That is precisely what I am referring to in these messages.

Who would appoint the senior members of the IRA to investigate IRA activities? Such an investigation would carry no validity whatever. Therefore, the church has to ensure that an investigation into this behaviour is done carefully, fully, and independently. Witnesses must be called, and the alleged perpetrators. Evidence must be gathered and the appropriate steps taken to root out this elephant from the churches.

Now, I do not know about you, but when I was growing up, it was customary not to speak of one particularly deadly disease — *cancer*. In fact, the word was seldom if ever used in polite conversation. People would speak of 'the big C, or 'the bad one,' or use some such term. However, they hardly ever use the word '*cancer*.' That is understandable, is it not? It is a horrible topic and a worse reality for too many people who have suffered from it. However, it is an elephant in the room.

Again, in polite society, respectable people will not

want to talk about *abortion*. It is not a nice topic of conversation, is it? In addition, ministers would not preach on this subject to respectable church people.

I remember once being told something like that about my Gospel preaching, that it was suitable only for street corners and mission halls, and that a respectable church is not the place for that kind of preaching; and another friend of mine was told exactly the same when he preached on abortion in a different denomination. Therefore, abortion, too, is a hush-hush subject of conversation or discussion. It, too, is an elephant in the room.

Nevertheless, I am not going to think about either of these two issues today. There is another issue falls into exactly the same category, and that is the issue of *bullying and spiritual abuse* in and by the churches.

I remember giving a little book that I wrote. 'Overcoming Bullying in School,' with a target readership of secondary school children; and when I spoke about this to a school principal whom I knew, he responded, saying that there is no bullying in his school. Very interesting, is it not?

During my academic research for my Master's degree, I read interviews of those who experienced bullying. I also read interviews of those in the organisations that were doing the bullying. One particular interview comes to mind. It was with a severely bullied employee who gave a graphic description of what happened to him. The manager of the same company said dismissively, 'There is no bullying in our place.' Two diametrically opposed views of the same workplace and of the same event.

I remember putting this same question to a very senior churchman. I asked him about bullying in and by the church, and what training was given to students for the ministry on this subject, and his response was the very same as the school principal and the company manager. There is no bullying in our church. So here we have an affirmation of bullying on the one hand, and then a complete denial by senior people in the same organisation, on the other, that there is any bullying among them. Very interesting, indeed, is it not?

A former principal of Union Theological College, Belfast, knew what he was talking about when he wrote about 'an age when many people have been abused and hurt by bad or dysfunctional church government.'[1] Did he experience this horrific

---

[1] Rev. J. Stafford Carson, cited in *'I will build my church.'* Thomas

behaviour? Did he dispense it? I do not know. But he acknowledged that church abuse is a common reality and experience of ministers and members of the Christian church today.

The two worst workplaces for bullying, according to research in the 1990s, were teaching and nursing. That changed a little bit as indicated by later research carried out twelve years ago. While these two professions were still high up in the list, prison officers and health professionals have replaced them. These two professions were far above the others that the research listed. You have it in the civil service; you have it in the police, and the army. You find it in industry; you find it in the charities, in banking, among nursing home workers; indeed, you find bullying wherever there are people.

That being the case, it should not come as any surprise to anyone to find that bullying is also present in the one place where you would least expect it to be, in the Christian Church, the community of love. It is there in the theologically liberal denominations, and it is rife in the conservative denominations. It is everywhere. In fact, the church is a religious organisation with which

---

Witherow. Ed. Jonathan Gibson. (Philadelphia: Westminster Seminary Press, 2021), opening printed page.

people work. They work in the church, that is, with people who profess to be Christians.

However, here is probably a new thing for you to consider. Do you know that bullies often run the denominations? In addition, did you know that the churches use bullying as a management tool to pull certain people into line with the establishment's policies?

I wish to do a few studies on this extremely rife subject because of the outright denial by senior churchmen that this happens within their jurisdiction. Not only do they deny this but most ministers also deny that this goes on. Why is that? Why do they deny the reality of this wicked behaviour within their own denominations? *First*, pride. 'Bullying would never go on in my church. We are Christians.' They deny the reality of this evil behaviour within their own denominations! They are too proud to admit that other colleagues treat their colleagues like dirt, as do their seniors. *Secondly*, they themselves are using bullying tactics against their own colleagues. In doing this, the bullies are bringing the church of Christ into disrepute within the church. Moreover, when this spills out into the public domain, they further bring the denomination into public disgrace in the world. They deny this, of course, but for those who have experienced it, and there are not a few, know that it is very real. And what does this do? It creates the deepest distrust among church members in the church leaders, and makes, even church members, doubt the truthfulness of their church leaders. *Thirdly,* those whom their colleagues have bullied are afraid to speak out and seek redress for what they did to them. The 'fear of man' silences them to the point where they internalise their hurt, thus leading to further emotional and mental problems down the line.

However, you might ask me, 'What has Scripture to say about this matter? You know, that is a very good question. Does Scripture have anything to say about this issue of bullying and spiritual abuse? Well, to answer this question, let me ask you some other questions. Does Scripture have anything to say about being kind and helpful to others? Or, about loving your neighbour? Or, about being respectful to God, and His servants? Has the Bible anything to say about thinking more highly of others than you do of yourself, or about esteeming others above yourself? Has Scripture something to say about these? Then, does our Lord say anything about knowing people *'by their fruits'*? On the other hand, did Paul write about maintaining our blood bought spiritual freedom in the face of all opposition? And about putting off the old man and putting on the new man? John wrote, *'Brothers, love one another.'* In the light of these verses, we can see that bullying is the polar opposite of these spiritual principles and virtues for Christian living.

Some Christians say that Scripture does not address the problem of spiritual abuse and bullying in and by

the church. Oh, I am afraid that those who say that kind of thing are obviously reading a different Bible from me!

However, you might ask me, 'What qualifications do you have to speak or preach on this subject'? This very good question that deserves an equally good answer. As well as being an ordained minister of the Gospel since 1979, *first*, my own denomination exposed me to many months of bullying between 1991 and 1993. So awful was this that it almost cost me my life, literally. When bullying descends to this level, all else involved in it is purely incidental. It nearly destroyed my family and me. *Secondly*, I researched this evil behaviour for my Master's degree, completing it in 1997. What the church had subjected me to was still very fresh in my memory, and I wanted to try to understand what it was that they did to me, and was it my fault. And *thirdly*, I have been providing support to several ministers from across the denominations who have been chosen for, what I call, 'the treatment.' I have spoken to many of these servants of Christ whose lives have been broken, men whose ministries have been ended (and not by their choice!), men whose marriages have been shipwrecked. The stress put on their families has been enormous. I have seen ministers' wives reduced to nervous wrecks, some having to spend months in psychiatric hospital as a direct result. I have heard the horror stories and have seen the tears. I have felt the pain of these manse families. I have not seen such anger such as I have witnessed from these servants of Christ, anywhere else!

Therefore, not only have I experienced this life-threatening and life-changing behaviour at the hands of the church, I have studied it to Master's degree level and have witnessed it again as a third party. Therefore, my knowledge of this is both experiential and academic. I think you will agree that I have a reasonable grounding in this subject.

For those of you who have been following my messages, you will know that I have been working my way through the Gospel according to Mark. My intention was to continue into chapter 8, having opened up the first seven chapters of Mark's Gospel. In fact, the message for the opening section of *Mark* 8 was in preparation.

However, something happened that stopped me proceeding with that series. God stepped in and impressed upon my heart the need to deal with this horrendous matter that pollutes Christ's Bride. In addition, because of the frequency of this devilish behaviour within the Christian Church today, I felt that it was time to focus on this issue for such time as God determines.

I know that this is going to be difficult for us all. It is going to be difficult *for me* because I will have to revisit the single most painful experience in my entire life. Nevertheless, it is going to be difficult *for you*, too, because these messages will force you to recognise just what ministers have to endure in their denominations. They may have been going through this very thing in the past months and years. This is nothing but barefaced, unadulterated bullying in and by the church. It will horrify you, the things you will hear. You will be shocked to think that those men who (used to) wear clerical collars would stoop to such a disgraceful level. They can, and they do. It will raise some unthinkable questions in your mind. It will confront you with issues that you never thought you would have to deal with.

To date, as a minister, you might be blaming yourself, for your church situation, as I did for mine. However, you would be very wrong to do that. 'What have I done that is so wrong?' you will ask yourself. 'Was I unfaithful to the Gospel? Did I not show pastoral care to the people? What is going on here?' I spent many sleepless nights trying to answer these awful questions, but to no avail. In addition, you ask these questions repeatedly, but you never get a satisfactory answer. They remain unanswered and often unanswerable questions.

The principle that I want you to grasp is this. Are you a minister? Are you a church member? Have you gone through this nightmarish experience? Are you going through this horror right now? Let me say this loud and clear – you are *not to blame* for the bullying that you are experiencing. Do you get that? You are *not to blame* for the abuse you are suffering. The bully is! The bully decided to target you for the treatment. No one is responsible for this but *the bully*. Moreover, while you, your wife, and your family are experiencing this awful ordeal, it is *not your fault*! I say to you again, *do not blame yourself. You* are not to blame for the bullying. The bully is. I would suggest to you to write this in big letters on your study wall and never forget this truth. No one ever puts his hand up and volunteers to be a victim of bullying. You become a victim of bullying because someone else has chosen to target you for 'the treatment'. It was *their choice, their decision, not yours*. If you put that statement on your wall, or keep it in the front of your Bible, you will find that by believing it to be true will be the first step towards recovery for you.

My dear brother or sister, minister or church member, you did not bring this on yourself. We will leave it there for the moment. There is much, much more to come. I trust that this will be revealing, and enlightening, and I trust it will also be pastoral for those of you who are *'stuck'* in that situation. It really is a matter of being *'stuck'* in that situation. I hope it will throw some biblical light on your situation, and also that these studies will point a way forward that will be helpful to you and aid your spiritual recovery, and ultimately for the recovery of the Christian churches from this devilish activity, and into usefulness in the spread of God's rule in this wicked world.

Prayer:

O, Lord, our gracious God, thank You that we can turn to Your Word and examine what You say to us in the Scriptures to find out about this terrible thing called bullying, that churches use as a tool to get their own way with their people.

Thank you that Your Word throws much light on this situation. Help us, oh God, as we study together, to find out what You say and what the way forward really is.

We ask these things in Jesus' Name, and for His sake. Amen.

2. Lack of Generosity Towards Others!

Leviticus 19:9,10

Anyone with any knowledge or experience of bullying knows that it only happens when basic human decency has been set aside. Bullying can only exist and prosper in the church when holiness of living, and of activity, is denied or non-existent. This reading from *Leviticus* 19 had the heading in my Bible, 'God commands holiness.'

Holiness and bullying abuse cannot co-exist in the same Body. That is utterly impossible. Where the church displays holiness, she will make every effort to remove every trace of bullying behaviour from her jurisdiction. Now the absence of holiness of life and living brings this kind of wicked behaviour into the church. Christians always need to be aware of what is actually happening within the church. When we look at it in the church, we will see that bullies can only succeed when and where the teaching of Scripture has been set aside.

We will see that there is nothing so incompatible with, or contradictory to, Christian character, as bullying behaviour. The two simply cannot co-exist in the one Body. It goes clean against everything we know the Christian character and holy living to be. It is without doubt godless behaviour, or the behaviour of the godless.

Yet senior churchmen in the churches today defend this wicked behaviour, as do their foot soldiers who operate at their command. In addition, they even glory in it! The thinking goes something like this: 'The fact that the church was strong enough to kick this man or that man out for whatever reason is great. We have the power of life and death over these men's ministries! We are the people.' Moreover, the churches despise those who dare to raise this as a reality within them, and they ghost them; they treat them as invisible, and regard them as troublemakers. The church does not listen to them, and they write off their views as odd, idiotic, silly. 'The Church would never behave like that,' they think.

Now, no one can be in any doubt that God requires decency and fairness in dealings amongst His own people. Moses wrote this portion of the Old Testament specifically for the children of Israel, to what we could call 'the city of God,' the people of God, the church in the Old Testament.

I ask you to have your Bible open at *Leviticus* 19 where we can see that God demands holiness from His people. And in the expression of that practical holiness, He demands generosity and consideration towards the poor and the vulnerable and the defenceless, vss 9,10. God's command for holiness prohibits stealing, or lying, or using God's Name falsely with regard to His people, vss 11,12. We see God's demand for honesty at all times there in v.13. There is to be no injustice in judgement done to a neighbour, and the taking of sides against the neighbour is wrong, v.15. This is what God requires. Indeed, God outlaws the sins of the tongue, such as gossiping and tale bearing, as is taking a stand against a neighbour, v.16.

Moving on to dealings with a brother, there is to be no heart hatred towards him, v.17. If he needs rebuke because of sin in his life, then that is proper. Nevertheless, you are not to take revenge against a brother or hold a grudge against him. On the contrary, you shall *'love your neighbour as yourself.'* Why? Because *'I am the Lord,'* v.18.

It is very interesting that in these verses, the phrase, *'I am the Lord,'* occurs fifteen times. That is the motivation for doing all these things. *'I am the Lord.'* I am the Self-existent One. I am the all-seeing, the all-hearing, the all-knowing God, the God of Abraham, Isaac, and Jacob, the covenant God. I am the God and Father of our Lord Jesus Christ. And it is with Me that you will have to do on the last day, not anybody else!' Not me, but God Himself.

Now God gave these laws, not to the world, but to His own people, v.2. God told Moses to speak to *all* the children of Israel, and here is the sum of His message: *'Be holy, for I am holy.'* Or it could be translated like this: *'Be holy ones, for I am holy.'* Moses had given many of these laws before. However, because the people had disobeyed them, Moses had to repeat them on several occasions to the people as a nation.

Now, it is clear from these verses that abusive, bullying, behaviour is very wrong. Look at vs 9 and 10 again.

'When you reap the harvest of your land, you shall not wholly reap the corners of your field, nor shall you gather the gleanings of your harvest. And you shall not glean your vineyard, nor shall you gather every grape of your vineyard. You shall leave them for the poor and the stranger. I am the Lord your God.'

Now, what is it that is required here? There is nothing complicated about this. This is easy to understand, but maybe a lot harder to do. God is speaking to our hearts. And what is required here? Nothing less than a spirit of generosity towards the poor, the vulnerable, the defenceless, such as, widows and orphans, and the foreigners who live among you. In short, all those who depend on others for their food and safety!

The Hebrew word translated *'poor'* in this version of the Bible (NKJV) also refers to the *'afflicted,'* the *'needy,'* the *'humble,'* the *'lowly.'* Interestingly, it also refers to the *'depressed'* because of their circumstances. We can see right away the application of this to those dear servants of Christ who have been broken and bruised and crushed by their churches, men who have been afflicted and plunged into depression because of their circumstances; that is who this is referring to. Moses uses the same word to describe them. How are they to be treated? With charitable acts of kindness and generosity; the church is to show them practical care and support. That is what holiness requires.

It is not about some second experience that you might have in your Christian journey. This is about real, everyday living out the Christian life in the eyes of your brothers and sisters in Christ and in the eyes of the world. Holiness requires nothing less than this. That is what the *'holy ones,'* you and I, Christian people like you and me, always strive to do. We are to love one another, not hate one another, not bully one another when it suits; not abuse one another when we do not get our own way. The Bible is clear from beginning to end – the great commandment to us is to love God first, and then we show the reality of our love for God when we love one another, when we love our brothers in Christ as we love ourselves. The last thing someone in that awful and most unenviable situation will need is further spiritual abuse and bullying, which is what he often gets. The church isolated men who had been in pastoral ministry after she subjected them to what I call 'the treatment.' The church side-lined them and ghosted them. They felt driven out into the wilderness where they met the wild beasts, the evil spirits, and the temptations of the devil himself. That is what the church did to them. And it is almost as if these men who do this kind of thing think, 'Stamp your foot on his neck and put as much pressure as possible on him so that he will not get up again or be involved in ministry.' That, in effect, is the attitude that lies at the heart of ungodliness.

As you know, ministers do not live in their own homes but usually in houses provided by the churches; they live in manses provided for them. Ministers, largely, depend on the good favour of members to remain there. They are also dependent, just like the poor, the needy, and the stranger, the widows and the orphans, on the generosity of the people for their livelihood. This is what God's holy people do to support God's servants. That is how the biblical church operates. Ministers just need enough to do their work and no more. They are to act in this way if they are to show practical responsibility towards other people. An over-arching sense of general brotherhood is to pervade everything they do in situations of difficulty. And you know, that is generally honoured more in the breach than in the observance. Therefore, generosity of spirit must be seen in all dealings with our brothers and sisters in Christ. Charitableness is to be clearly visible, so that the world will say, 'See how these Christians love one another.'

However, the churches break this law when ministers bully and abuse their peers. Moreover, it happens. I would not be dealing with this issue now were this not a reality within the churches. It is happening in Northern Ireland, and across in Great Britain. I know what is happening in at least one Anglican diocese in England. Friends informed me that bullying abuse is a real problem among the churches in Kenya, and in Spain, where jealousy and rigid competitiveness are the rule of the day.

When the situation arises where a minister finds himself in difficulties, his colleagues must then come to his aid and help him generously and wholeheartedly. They are not to gang up against him just to keep in with the denomination's 'ruling classes;' and the 'ruling classes' *do* rule the church! They are not to do that. Christ forbids all elders to lord it over the flock of God!

I am not advocating here the promotion of any kind of buddyism within the church. There is far too much of that going on at the present anyway. I am not talking about that. Nor am I talking about the in-groups, the cabals, the cliques, and so on, that abound within the church as visible. They have always been there and they always will be. They have always run the church. This small cabal of people have always determined the direction of the church. I am not talking about that.

What I am referring to is the establishment of a true brotherhood among God's people. That is what holiness demands. Unless a minister has become apostate, and denied the faith or become immoral in his living, his peers should support him, not abuse or bully and ill-treat him. Nor are they to crush and traumatise him. They are to be supported *by them* – *love one another. 'Love your neighbour as you love yourself.'*

In addition, it is the very denial of the law of God when they do the opposite, when they mete out ill-treatment instead of showing gracious consideration. On top of this, the Old Testament pronounced the fiercest judgements on those who do His prophets any harm (*Psalm* 105:15). The church should never target the true ministers of the Gospel for bullying, or abuse, or any such treatment. This must never happen. The world will do that well enough by itself.

It does not need the church, Christians, or ministers to help it pursue its evil plans and policies.

This happens in denominations today, where people are 'ganged up against,' targeted for 'the treatment.' Even the purest denominations destroy ministers!

Are you in that unenviable position today? If you are, do you know why? Let me tell you. Church bullies have targeted you for this 'treatment.' Instead of targeting you for generous treatment, they specifically targeted you for bullying and spiritual abuse. This was no accident, nor was it an unplanned thing. They had been planning this action for weeks or months before. They watched your every move, and they noted your every word. They monitored whom you keep company with and what you said. Then, with the precision of an Exocet missile, they took aim and fired their missile at you, the predetermined target, and they hit right where it would do maximum damage. That is how they operate!

The *modus operandi* of these people is the same as the IRA terrorists who still lurk about and still operate in Northern Ireland. Like these terrorists, they targeted you for some time, believe me. They had all their plans in place, just awaiting the right time to strike. They did, they hit you, and you felt it. They 'holed you beneath the water line' and down you went. They hit you with devastating accuracy and consequences, and you did not even know what struck you. Generosity? Brotherhood? Compassion for the poor and the needy? Not a trace of it.

What made it a thousand times worse was this: it was your colleagues in the ministry who fired this Exocet missile of bullying and spiritual abuse at you. The world did not fire it; nor did the enemy. Your fellow ministers in the church fired it! In military terms, this was a *blue on blue* incident, carried out with merciless accuracy; and they got you. It registered a victory on the dashboard of the attackers. Like our Lord Jesus Christ, you and I were wounded *'in the house of our friends.'* The strike of an enemy is bad. However, when so-called friends did it, it is infinitely worse. In addition, it stays with you for life. There is no 'get out of jail free' card for you on this one. Generosity? Brotherly love? Compassion? Understanding? Hardly. True brotherhood and practical generosity were wholly absent in their dealings with you at that time and afterwards.

That is what many of Christ's servants are experiencing in the church today, many of them, I say to you! You might say, 'But I have not heard that before.' No, you have not. Not from them, at least. Why? Because they are scared stiff to raise their voices to complain of the abusive treatment that they have been subjected to, in and by the church. There has been a silent holocaust where the church has culled the servants of Christ in sacrifice to whatever god the churches worship! The system demanded sacrifice, and it got it!

In closing this chapter, let me ask you a few pointed questions. How are you treating your minister? Do you pray for him? Do you pray *earnestly* for him? Do you give him encouragement and generous support? Do you go out of your way to encourage him at every opportunity? Do you tell him that what he said in the sermon meant something to you? 'It stuck in my heart and I have some thinking to do.' Have you said to him about how helpful you find his sermons? Or, about how helpful you find his pastoral visitation. Do you stand by him when times are tough for him, when the dogs are baying for his blood, when the wolves are at his door – and we all get tough times in church work? Do you draw alongside him to comfort and support him?

Minister, how are you treating your Gospel-preaching colleagues? With utmost respect? Do you show them the generosity of spirit that they need in the midst of their trials? Or, when he is down, do you join with the others and stamp your feet on his neck to make sure he will never get up again? What would your colleagues say about your attitude to them, especially those in tough situations? Would you get a good report from them? Or, would their report be an unmentionable one? I say to you, search your own heart and search it deeply.

In conclusion, pray for Christ's faithful servants in all the Christian, that is, evangelical, denominations, especially those who are facing difficulties. Pray for those evangelicals in the theologically liberal denominations, for they stand in need of God's grace and protection in a mighty way. May I ask you to pray for me as I preach on this vile and vitally important subject? I have no doubt that Satan will be aroused.

We must seek God's protection from this bitterest of enemies. He is there! He is active. He will come to us. He will visit you if you have found this agreeable to you as you look at the state of your own heart; but he will come to you with devastating effect. Therefore, we need to seek the Lord that He will build a hedge around us; that His almighty arm will be our protection, and that we might find in Him the defence that we need. Pray, and seek the Lord. Seek Him earnestly. Seek Him persistently. Seek Him until you know that He has heard your cry. The best thing we can do now, as I close this chapter, is to pray to the same God whose grace and protection we need so much.

Prayer:

O Lord, our gracious, loving Father, we come to You in all our nakedness and in all our helplessness, in all our vulnerability. Lord, You know the conditions that Your servants are working in at this time, being starved of the support and encouragement they need within their congregations and within their denominations.

Lord, we ask that You will turn their hearts to Yourself; remind them that they are not on their own, even though they might feel that way. Assure them, Lord, that there are people out there who know what it is like and who will come alongside them to give them the help and the support they so desperately need. We pray, Lord, that You will drive back the forces of darkness from the Church of Jesus Christ, here in this land.

Your church, Lord, is to be found in all the Christian evangelical denominations. Lord, look in pity upon Your Church, and be pleased to strengthen Your servants who are faithful to You. Lord, turn the tide. Drive back the powers of darkness. And may the glorious light of the everlasting Gospel shine brightly once again through the Bride of Christ.

For it is in Jesus' Name that we pray. Amen.

3. Lies and Deception!

Leviticus 19:11,12.

We are looking at a couple of verses, again from *Leviticus* 19:11,12. It is clear from even a casual reading of Scripture that any lack of generosity towards another is wrong. The three words, *'love one another,'* sum up the whole message of the Bible. Our love for God comes first while our love for one another comes second and sums up the second table of the Law of God.

We saw last time that what Scripture demands is a spirit of whole-hearted generosity with a view to helping and supporting each other. It is about going the extra mile and helping those who are in need, as Jesus told us. It is about drawing alongside those at the front line of the battle against Satan and sin. It is about being courageous enough to stand out from the crowd and identify with the brother who is 'getting it hard' at this time? I wonder what verses 11 and 12 can teach us.

Well, the teaching of the entire Bible is for a redeemed people, including the book of *Leviticus*. It is for people who were delivered, rescued, ransomed, and brought out of Egypt under the leadership of Moses by God's mighty hand. *Leviticus* is for a redeemed people and teaches them how to live to please their great Redeemer, God, and to serve Him. It is about how they are to live and worship God. It is about holiness before God and man.

Moreover, what does God require of man? What does He require of *you*? Obedience to His revealed will; the familiar words of Shorter Catechism, 39. *Micah* 6:8 explains this more fully. *'He has shown you, Oh man, what is good. What does God require of you but to do justly, to love mercy, and to walk humbly with your God.'* *To do justly.* In other words, you never act or behave in an unjust way towards anyone else. *To love mercy.* In other words, you are not out for revenge or retaliation. *To walk humbly with your God.* There should be no arrogance or self-righteousness in your dealings with others. In other words, in line with *'the whole counsel of God'* we are to *love our neighbour.* How? *'As you love yourself.'* It is about showing kindness driven by Christian love for one another.

I think that is clear, simple, and easily enough understood. It is saying that stealing, dealing falsely, and lying to or about one another, are wrong, and these must stop. These sins must not even be mentioned among the people of God. Look at it like this: do you want someone to steal your goods, your name, and your reputation? Then do not steal those of others. Do you want people to deal falsely with you? No? Then do not deal falsely with them, do not believe or act on those falsehoods. Do you want other people to lie about you? Then, do not lie about them? Do not even let this be mentioned among the people of God. It is that simple.

However, stealing is about much more than taking another's possessions. It includes robbing a man of his God-given ministry, something that all the churches have done many times. Many, many men have found this. God gave them their ministry and He equipped and called them; and now the church has snatched this ministry from them. Stolen.

A former minister stood in my home, and with outstretched arms said, 'I lost everything. They have taken everything from me.' Is that what the Bible understands as stealing? What they took was not theirs to take. That is stealing. The Law of God forbids that kind of behaviour. You know your Shorter Catechism 75, do you not? What does it say? The eighth commandment *forbids whatever does or may justly hinder our own or our neighbour's wealth or outward estate.* We must not do that kind of thing!

Has your behaviour had that affect? Have you acted in such a way towards your neighbour, your colleague in the ministry? He has lost what was most precious to him, his God-given ministry. Have you taken that from him? Have you acted by foul means to rob your neighbour?

Now what ought you to have done? Well, the Shorter Catechism 74 gives us the answer. You are *to 'further your neighbour's wealth and outward estate,'* not diminish it. Have you done that? Where is the evidence? Show me someone to whom you have acted in such a way as to further their well-being! Yes, as Christians, these things belong to the old man, and he has been put to death in Christ.

However, the big question is, and you know this, do these sins still raise their ugly head in your life and in the life of your church? Is that happening today? Do Christians steal today? Do Christians, do the people of God, deal falsely with other people? You know that no one will steal from another who does not first think deceitfully about him in his heart, and then convince himself that to take from them what is rightfully theirs is OK. And they do it. Do Christians lie today? What about inside the church?

Are lies being told inside the church? Do Christ's servants lie in order to put another man down? Do ministers steal from others? Do they deal falsely with others, especially with colleagues? Do ministers lie to and about one another? Do they spread rumours and untruths about others because they cannot bear to see them getting on? Do ministers suggest to others not to associate with those the church has destroyed, on the basis that 'dirt sticks'? 'Have nothing to do with that man, because "dirt sticks," and it could stick to you.' It could jeopardise your future career in the ministry. And you do not want that now, do you? So stay away from such people. Do not even recognize them.' Are such men to be shunned? Are they to be ghosted? That happens.

We were at a concert at a local theatre not too long ago when the conductor thanked everybody for their contributions; a young friend of mine, a good musician in his own right, played a vital part in the proceedings. But the conductor omitted to mention him in the thanks, and treated him as if he was invisible; he ghosted him. That happens.

What strange, self-contradictory things these are! 'These are awful things to ask questions about,' you might say. I agree; they are awful questions. It ought never to enter the minds of Christians to ask such probing, searching, and sobering questions. However, someone must ask them in today's faithless churches. Once you get that understanding of what it is really like to be a minister in such a church setting, then you will grasp what I am trying to say.

You remember Moses was writing in *Leviticus* to *all* the people of God. He gets that spot on, does he not? He would never have written these words to the Old Testament church were these things not going on, would he? Paul would never have written his epistles to the churches in the first century had there not been problems in them. Moreover, when these commandments, these divine requirements that God says are to be met, are obeyed, blessing flows. Blessing follows those who surrender their lives to God and to His Word, and not to anything else.

However, these conditions are not being met in the churches today, hence the state of the church and consequently the state of the nation in which we live. Problems within the church are enormous. However, nobody seems to see them.

What is bullying abuse?[2] First, what it is not. It is not abuse when the spiritual leader, who has the responsibility to make final decisions, uses his best judgment and chooses to go against your opinions. That is not abusive. However, it is abusive if someone uses their opposing view to devalue their spirituality. That is different. It is not abusive when a Christian, whether he is a leader or not, confronts another Christian because of sin in his life, some

[2] Johnson, D, and VanVonderen, J. *The Subtle Power of Spiritual Abuse* (Minneapolis: Bethany House Publishers, 1991), 24.tim

wrongdoing, or mistake, he may have made that he must correct. That is not abusive. However, it is abusive when a man's friends break him with no hand of help offered to him. That is different.

You see, when you have to confront a brother or a sister in Christ about their walk with the Lord, the objective is to bring them back into line again with what Scripture teaches. It is to heal, save, and restore. Moreover, if it was discipline in any sense, the expectation of restoration is always present. Well, in my own experience and in the experience of men I have talked to, that never came to any one of them! They hounded and destroyed, and 'disciplined' – dare I use the word? – them, but the church took no steps to restore them to fellowship and to usefulness in the church's ministry.

This is very important because leaders must take decisions that affect the church. Not all the decisions are popular or even correct, nor do they please everyone, and not all of them will guarantee you your Christmas card at the end of the year. Nevertheless, they are mere decisions, and no more. Where the bullies overstep the mark is when they take or use decisions to get at the targeted person with a view to disadvantaging him. Or where the decision is intended to disadvantage a group of people later on. That is abusive. In addition, that leads inescapably to bullying and does great and lasting damage. If the unpopular decision causes deep hurt and distress, then the leader who took that decision must also take every step to explain the process and the reasons for it and to ensure the healing and restoration of the hurt individual. Not to do so shows that bullying was at work at the time, and that an ulterior motive or motives were at play. The absence of follow-up personal support proves my case. This is bullying, and it is not on!

In Spain, signs appear at the *Renfe* train stations, reading, 'Prohibido crusar las vias,' translated as 'Do not cross the tracks.' Bullying, under any guise, always crosses the line!

Now, here is the point. Spiritual abuse is a trap. It traps anyone and everyone in the vicinity. Now, traps, by their very nature, are usually hidden from view; they are not obvious things. But the abusers are as much trapped by their own unhealthy beliefs and actions, by their own wickedness and corruption, as those they abuse. In counselling, there is a term: 'hurt people hurt people.' Those who inflict hurt on those they associate with are themselves, hurting. Bullies could well be hurting inwardly and they display their hurt by hurting other people.

Now, let me say this: that is not a 'get out of jail free' card for them, mind you, but it is a statement of fact. These people are hurting so badly that they do not know they are hurting. Nor could they care less that they are hurting others. They could even have been hurt by the very people they are now protecting and cooperating with against a colleague! The hurt and damage they inflict on others is inexcusable and they must repent immediately. The harsh reality of life is that bad things do happen to good people. That is just life in this fallen world.

Nevertheless, I want you to examine your Christian life as you read these chapters. I designed these sermons to get you thinking about your Christian life and about your walk with Christ, and about your church's life. Is your church stealing a man's gifts of preaching and pastoring, robbing him of these precious God-given gifts? Then let it stop. You are stealing from Christ's Bride, and that is serious. Maybe you could raise this with your church leaders.

Is your church dealing falsely with others, unjustly, wickedly, and in a corrupt manner? Then this must stop immediately. Perhaps you could raise this with your church leaders.

Is the church lying about what is really happening 'behind the counter,' as I would put it? Then, she must come clean by owning up to both her innocent and her deliberate mistakes. You could raise this with the leaders.

The churches must repent of their sins, their wickedness, and their corruptions. They must, hand on heart, confess this before the Holy God who knows all things, that they have acted wickedly. They must repent of these sins and take steps to restore those that they have damaged. For if the church refuses to repent of her sins how can she ever expect the world to repent of its sins? And the greatest, most urgent need in both church and world today is for a deep, heartfelt repentance before the holy God whom they have offended, and a return to Him forthwith.

Oh, these are difficult messages to read, and I would not want anyone to go away with the idea that I am having a go at the churches. I am not. I am concerned about the spiritual well-being of the churches, and particularly the protection of the servants of Christ within the churches. It is a rough world, and it is a tough world, but it is also tough for solid evangelicals in the churches. They do not listen to them, nor regard them; and they are invisible. So, I say to you again, pray for the servants of Christ. Pray earnestly for them, that God will keep them faithful to Him at all times, faithful to Scripture. By being faithful to the Word, they are being faithful to God and they are being faithful to your souls as well.

I trust that this has been something of a blessing and a challenge, a rebuke and an encouragement to you.

Prayer:

O Lord our God and gracious Father, we come humbly and broken before You. We know what Your Word requires, but we have failed. You have told us not to steal. Yet we have taken from others what is not rightfully ours to take. You have told us to deal honestly and justly with other people. We have failed there, too. Lord, You know our hearts and our lives. You know we have failed You on every count. So, forgive us, Lord. Forgive me, Lord. And forgive those who are reading these sermons. Bring us to true repentance that we might receive your mercy and your forgiveness and full restoration to communion with the Lord, and with His Bride.

For we ask all these mercies in Jesus' Name. Amen.

4. No Holiness, Much Bullying!

Leviticus 19:13,14

What is the Church of Jesus Christ? It is a living organism, or entity, or Body that has become a Christian organisation within which people work. They work in the church, that is, with people who profess to be Christians. She is a Body of the redeemed, together with their children. She consists of sinners who were once the enemies of God and who are now reconciled to God. Because their relationship with God has been fundamentally changed through faith in Jesus Christ alone, so has how they live in this world. Their life has undergone a fundamental and radical change. In other words, their newfound religion has changed them. They now live moral lives. People see the difference in how they live now to how they lived before they were converted.

And what is it that brings about this fundamental change in ethics or morality? It is the Gospel and nothing but the Gospel. Dr P. T. Forsyth emphasised something very important here. He emphasised what he called 'ethical religion.' Now, many people today use the terms 'ethics' and 'morality' interchangeably. Besides, these have their basis in the law of God. There is something called 'the right,' and there is something called 'the wrong.' This is so important because if our faith in the risen Christ does not change our lives, then we have adopted the wrong religion. It is *not* the Christian faith. In addition, the proof of our religion lies in how we live our lives day by day, and how we treat other people. If we do not care for our everyday living then we are not Christians! That is a very bold statement, so can I say it again? Please do not miss this. If we do not care for our everyday living, then we have not got or entered into the Christian faith, and the Christian faith has not entered into us. God said to the children of Israel, the Church of the Old Testament, through Moses, *'Be holy, for I am holy, says the LORD.'* That means that known unholy behaviour and living is not of God. It is *of the world*. Deliberately working to harm another is to live in opposition to Christ.

Leviticus 19:13 points us to this very truth. Does Moses tell the children of Israel, and therefore us, that it is OK to cheat on your neighbour? What does he say? Well, he starts with a very strong negative, the Hebrew word *lo*. That is exactly the same word that God uses throughout the Ten Commandments. 'You shall have *no* other gods before Me, you shall *not* take God's Name in vain, and you shall *not* murder or steal or commit adultery, or bear false witness, or covet.' They both cover the same, strong prohibition, the same word being used in either case.

Therefore, what Moses says here to the children of Israel is this: 'no cheating.' What does he mean by that? Scripture also uses this word for violating another, whether physically, verbally, or spiritually. It means to put undue pressure on or to defraud or wrong another person. It means no bullying. Furthermore, bullies do all these God-forbidden things; that is their *modus operandi*. That is how they operate day by day. Putting pressure on someone is their favourite ploy. They love to squeeze or crush another person. I have seen that with my own eyes and felt it in my own body. No one must do this to another, under any circumstances. It tells us that there is no justification whatever for this wicked behaviour, at least not in the church.

Nonetheless, it happens. It happens in the church. It is going on as you read this chapter. These bullies, these psychopaths, are crushing men. They are doing to others what the Cross did to our Lord Jesus Christ. You remember, He was crushed. He was bruised. He was broken. That is what the bullies did to us! People who crush another are re-crucifying Christ. Ministers have used this very word when they described what the church did to them. They said to me, *'they crucified me.'* That is exactly what they did.

In a most painful way, we are sharing in His sufferings. It is not redemptive; but it is certainly analogous to it. Those who do this are acting in clear disobedience to the Word of God, the Law of God.

So be warned if you are doing that, if you are giving your colleague in the ministry a hard time. If you, as a member of the church, are giving your minister a hard time, be warned. You will have God to contend with when you crush one for whom Christ died.

Consequently, there is to be no cheating. That is a strong prohibition. Then Moses says, 'there is to be no robbing.' Moses uses the same strong Hebrew negative, and he says, no robbing. He has ruled this out in vss 11,12 that we looked at in the last chapter. Also, raising this matter again is quite important, and we must not miss the significance of this. He is raising this issue again within a couple of verses, because it is clear that robbing and stealing are a big issue for the people of God, and this goes on within the people of God. Could you believe it? It was going on in the Old Testament Church, the people of God, Israel.

Besides, because the Lord Jesus Christ did not come to destroy the law but to keep it, this prohibition still applies today. Robbing and stealing are wrong. For by robbing, you are separating someone from what is rightfully theirs. They may have got it by the work of their hands or as a gift, but it is theirs. They own it; it is their treasured possession. Moreover, you have no right whatsoever to tear them from their possession.

What is the application of this teaching? What is the principle here to guide us? Well it is this: You are not to tear anyone away from their Gospel work without very good reason. To be set upon by robbers is a terrible thing. God outlaws this. God prohibits having what is precious to you taken from you ruthlessly. When that happens, you have been plundered, and you have been left with nothing because they have taken the most important thing you had from you. It is about tearing from a man what God had given him for his work of service. Equally, they did not do that graciously, either. Well, how can someone tear something away from you *graciously*? It is impossible. No grace or mercy was involved or shown, and the actions that the bullies took showed no compassion or kindness.

Now, they did this behind the 'closed doors' of the church. They robbed men of their ministry; and with that went their livelihood, their home, and their health in every case. This put their marriages under awful strain; and damaged their families almost irreparably.

These are the dreadful human effects of bullies and spiritual abusers within the Christian Church. As well, Moses continues using the same strong negative word, *lo,* to forbid the depriving a neighbour of his wages, the reward for his work, until morning. At that time in Israel's history, employers were to pay wages each evening. To delay payment until the morning would be illegal and cause distress to the family. It is as if they had taken his wages from him when he needed them most. Moses says that God's people are not to do that kind of thing under any circumstances.

Yet ministers are facing life without income, and without a home. Some good men are struggling on state benefits because they are unfit to work. Strong, able men thrown on the scrap heap. Worthless. Good for nothing. Furthermore, the church did that!

What an utter waste that is in the Body of Christ! What wickedness it took for anyone to do that and to have that action on their consciences! Those who do such things are facing unspeakable wrath from the Holy God. Law-breaking and spiritual abusers is second nature to bullies and spiritual abusers. They care nothing for God or His law or His Word.

V.14 ups the ante here by adding the example of the *deaf* and the *blind*. Who are they? Well, they are people who have no comeback against those who deal harshly with them. If you come and hit a blind man, he cannot see you and he does not know where to retaliate if he wanted to. If you shouted abusive things at a deaf man, he cannot hear what you are saying. Therefore, he has no comeback, either! It is as if they targeted him simply because he had no comeback.

What is the application of this? The application here is that the victims or targets of bullying have no comeback or appeal against immoral decisions taken concerning them. That is bad! That is offensive to God. To abuse or to bully in any way the defenceless, the weak, or the powerless, is utterly abhorred by the God of the Bible. That is the guiding principle here. They feel at a total loss as to what to do; they are confused, and in church circles when a group of men take a life-changing decision about another, the victim is defenceless. He is weak and powerless, just like the deaf and the blind man.

The principle here is the same. They have nowhere to go! They have no appeal that they can make. They are just like the deaf and the blind; they can do nothing to remedy their situation. In addition, Moses prohibits this in the strongest terms; *'you shall not*' do these things. This is wrong. This is most unacceptable, and without any justification. This is exploitation of a wicked kind. Taking advantage of another by foul means is wrong. Even amongst thieves, there is honour. But sadly, amongst ministers, even this care seems to be absent.

What they do is they put an obstacle before them. That is thoroughly unfair. Paul tells us that masters are to deal justly with their servants, (*Ephesians* 6:9 and *Colossians* 4:1). Ministers are servants who work under their masters, the 'ruling class.' Therefore, to treat them well and with justice and consideration is what is required of them. They are not to *lord it over* anybody else. Why are they not to do that? Two reasons. *First*, these servants of the Gospel are divine image bearers. They are God's handiwork, made in the image and likeness of God. *Secondly*, here is a mighty motivation to do what is right: *'I am the Lord.'* Why is that a mighty motivation? Because of the fear of the Lord?

The problem with bullies and spiritual abusers is that they have no fear of the Lord. How could they, for if they had, they would never do that kind of thing. They do not know what the fear of the Lord is! They have no respect for Him; therefore, they do not intend to obey His law. They are what the theologians call 'antinomians.' That word has two parts: *anti*, (against), and *nomos* (law), in the Greek. They are against law, against the instruction of God. They are against the doctrine or teaching of Scripture that God has set forth in His Word.

Rev. Richard Baxter (1615-1691) is arguably the greatest of the English Puritans, and he spent most of his long life exposing and opposing the dangers of antinomianism. What a problem that is in the church today. Now that God has saved us by grace through faith, the argument goes, we are eternally secure, and therefore we can live however we please. That is the reasoning behind antinomianism. That is also the reasoning behind bullying in and by the church. These bullies claim to be Christ's servants; therefore, they do not need to worry about how they live. They are eternally secure. They can treat people any old way, and still claim to be living for Christ and in His service.

The righteousness that God delights in does five very important things in us. I will only give you the headings but these are deserving of further exploration.

The righteousness that God delights in, *first*, pervades our whole life. *Secondly*, it purifies all our habits. *Thirdly*, it ennobles all our actions. *Fourthly*, it stamps our character with goodness.

And *fifthly*, it stamps conduct with integrity. How useful it would be to study and tease these out in your own time.

As I close, true biblical religion is for daily life. It is not just for church meetings and prayer meetings, Bible studies or missionary meetings. It is for every place and every moment of our lives. True religion sanctifies our manhood. It uplifts all actions; it exalts and graces all our aims with true dignity. We tend to forget these things. Nonetheless, that is true religion. False religion could not care less about these things.

Bullies are into false religion big time, believe it or believe it not. Yes, they may stand in a pulpit on a Sunday. And, yes, they may conduct prayer meetings. Yes, they may visit the people. Yes, they may preach at evangelistic missions and rallies. They may do all these things. Still, the way they behave is reminiscent of false religion. They do not care who they destroy and what damage they leave behind. In fact, they glory in the destruction of others, so long as they retain their power and their position.

Yes, they do destroy people! Oh, if you could hear the things I have heard, and see what I have seen, you would understand what I am saying. It you could see the damage, the wreckage that these people have left within the church, and how these men are outside the church, it would abhor you. They behave like the psychopaths that they are. When they do enormous damage to others, they can still go to bed at night and sleep soundly. What they did does not take a fizz out of them.

Why is that? Because they do not see the wrong that they did; nor do they judge their actions by the law of God, or by the grace of Christ. They just do not care so long as they are OK.

One more thing and I am done. Bullies do not fear God, v.14. Forget about their profession. Forget about their education. Forget about their ordination and qualifications, and forget about their position. *Bullies do not fear God.* For no one who fears God will ever mistreat another person. They will never cheat on them nor lie about them nor steal from them, nor gossip about them. Never.

Also, just as bullying and holiness cannot co-exist in the same body, nor can bullying and the fear of God. For bullies, there is no fear of God before their eyes. Therefore, they trash people at will. They do it under the cover of 'caring for the church.' They try to persuade onlookers that they are doing it for the health and well-being of the church. What an utter contradiction, if not blasphemy, that very attitude is!

Brothers and sisters, I say to you, be alert to what is going on in your church. For this evil is there. It is lurking behind a pseudo-spirituality. It lurks behind religion and orthodoxy, and morality and niceness. It is there!

Oh, beware of those who are so nice to you. There is an old saying that I was brought up with, which said, *'So and So is too sweet to be wholesome.'* Be watchful, be vigilant; and be courageous enough to raise the matter of church bullying with your leaders, and urge them to take it up with the church authorities.

This has been painful to deliver and to hear. I am sure some of you are saying, 'I cannot believe what I am

hearing from this man.' Let me assure you, this is the truth. This is what is going on behind the closed doors of many churches today.

Consequently, I say to you, pray for, support, and encourage your minister. Stand publicly with your minister and against those who are out to destroy him. Do not let anyone, be he a neighbour, a minister, or some respected person in the community, bring him down. He is too precious to you. Furthermore, he is precious to God. In fact,

God views him as the 'apple of His eye,' and woe betide anybody who touches the 'apple of His eye.'

These are big issues, and they are very painful. Yet, I must address these issues in the public domain, and people must take these matters seriously. The sad thing is that bullies always refuse to believe that these things are happening under their watch. Unbelievably, they refuse to believe these things, because they, in all likelihood, are the bullies within their church.

Prayer:

Our Father, Your Word comes to us like a 'hammer that breaks the rock in pieces.' Lord, You have touched us again. You have spoken to our situation. You have enlightened our minds. You have opened our eyes so that we can see what others refuse to see.

We pray that You will keep us all safe because the bullies do not like to be exposed, just like their master, the devil. He does not like to be exposed and held up in his true colours. So, Lord, the bullies will retaliate. They will react. And they will do it in a most secretive, underhand, and malicious way.

We pray that You will keep Your good hand on us, and Your mighty hand of protection on me. Lord, be with Your faithful servants, and use them to bring new life to Your church.

We ask this in Jesus' Name. Amen.

5. Injustice and Gossip?

Leviticus 19:15,16

Bullying/spiritual abuse is one of the most horrible experiences that anyone can endure. It is a dreadful issue, and it is one, certainly the bullying part of it, that is in the news with increasing frequency, exposing people who are accused of bullying behaviour towards their staff, and also the bullying that we know about on young gymnasts and footballers. It is happening right across Europe, and in the USA, in Canada, and in Australia. Christian ministers have informed that it is in the churches of Kenya and in the Philippines. It is rampant in GB churches and here in Northern Ireland. It is a massive problem which no one seems to want to acknowledge. However, facts do not cease to exist because we ignore them!

We have talked about the big elephant in the room, that everyone knows is there but no one wants to talk about, or better still, have it removed from the room. We have all heard of domestic violence, child abuse, racial abuse, and even animal abuse. And the very sound of these words horrifies us, because it involves wanton cruelty. Spiritual abuse falls into exactly the same category. It is abuse and cruelty inflicted on members of the Christian Church by other members and officers of the church. They are in the same category. Yet there is no outrage from the churches against such wickedness, is there? The churches administer this cruelty, and we must deplore and condemn it in the strongest possible terms. Every decent Christian must work to outlaw it in the churches.

We are looking at the Holiness Code section of *Leviticus*, and here Moses tells us that legal abuse is another area where we see abuse and this, too, is wrong. The deliberate withholding of justice from your neighbour, v.15, is a form of abuse. We often hear that 'justice delayed is justice denied.' IRA terrorists murdered my brother, yet we still have not had justice. The state has denied us justice because it wants to protect these 'community bullies'! Here Moses tells us that that is legal abuse.

Another thing that Moses outlawed here is court abuse, whether secular or ecclesiastical. In Israel at that time, both forms of court amounted to the same thing. In the context of the church, where there is a system of courts, they must not deny justice to anyone for any reason. Justice must not only *be* done in church courts, but be *seen* to be done; and truth and righteousness must always be evident. When the church denies justice, that, in itself, is a form of spiritual abuse. The abuse of power, of position, of authority, and of the individual at the receiving end, is a dreadful experience. What makes the situation worse is that the spiritual abuser has the weight of ecclesiastical authority behind what he is doing!

We know that in the sphere of law, *justice is blind*, and *there is no grace in law*. That is what they tell us! However, when someone of standing, someone well connected or well in with the church establishment appears in the church courts, they are dealt with more favourably than anyone else! Moses says that they must deal with them according to *righteousness*. There is to be no favouritism shown to anyone. Likewise, because someone is poor, weak, or defenceless, and who is not well in with the decision makers and judges, does not mean that they are to deal with them shoddily or unjustly. And just because a man is one of standing with the church community, a 'mighty person' v.15, does not mean that he is to get off with murder, so to speak.

Yet, that happens! A minister can rewrite history by referring to an acknowledged terrorist as 'a man of peace,' and the church is happy with that. Inversely, someone who preaches the Gospel and seeks church reform according to the Scriptures, well, he is repudiated and removed. I think people can see that there are double standards in church decision-making.

Now, such a thing is not to be done or mentioned among the people of God. They are to be above that kind of thing. Did you know that in church circles, letters can be written and signatures forged by a senior Church official in a bid to do another minister down? When the other minister confronted the Church official about this situation, the first minister's card was marked and he was forced out! Is that justice?

Moses, then, proceeds to speak of sins of the tongue. These two things, strange as it may seem, are linked. He links this with the judgement that we were talking about before and about court appearances. At first, I could not see this strange connection, but it is there. When I picked up the commentary on *Leviticus* by my first Hebrew teacher at Queens University, Belfast, Dr Gordon Wenham, he makes an excellent point when he writes concerning witnesses at court,

'They must not spread gossip that will bring a man into court, or worse still, accuse him falsely of crimes that bring the death penalty.'

The churches today, thankfully, cannot impose the death penalty as it was with them long ago. That said they have replaced the death penalty with bullying and spiritual abuse. Loose talk costs lives. False talk, gossip, and untruths cost dearly. Being innocent and bringing an innocent man into the church courts, sadly the church leaders believe false talk no matter how out of line it is with the truth. Judges in church courts, that is, the elders, believe themselves to be infallible when they come to a judgement, and when they make the decision, that is it, and you can do nothing about it. They never make mistakes nor come to wrong judgements; that is why you have no appeal against those decisions. This is the Protestant church's equivalent of Rome's papal infallibility and the infallibility of the church. Talebearers are very dangerous people. The point is that bullies believe talebearers, especially if they are evangelicals. The bullies and their talebearers do untold damage to Christ's cause in this world. Moreover, everyone knows it goes on!

After elders' meetings, even before the minister arrives back home, the business is out in the congregation! Church prayer meetings can so easily degenerate into gossip shops where they hear the news of who is sick or in hospital, and anything else that might tickle ears. The word spreads like wildfire.

Gossip is wrong. It breaks the law of God and it damages people. The reality is that bullying depends on gossip and tale bearing among God's people, v.16. Oh, how much they glory in doing someone down; and the juicier the gossip, the better! I think churches have a term for it – *fama clamosa*; rumours, tale-bearing, gossip, chin-wagging.

Now, just imagine how much damage this does to someone who is brought before a church court. Some ministers are well known as gossips. I will always be very wary of ministers who seem to know everything about everyone.

While in regular pastoral ministry, there were two ministers who had all the news, all the gossip, about everyone. This alarmed me as a young minister. Do ministers do that kind of thing? Yes, they do. At ministers' meetings, the latest news does the rounds. It is told to show sympathy with the poor soul who is the subject of the gossip. It is to ask for prayer and concern. However, it is still gossip! Tales are still being told! What is more, those listening take their 'holy gossip' as 'gospel.' How do they get it? They dig in order to get the juicy bits of the story on the minister they have targeted! What they discover does not even have to be true. They make it their business to get the latest news, be it true or false, it does not matter.

People who do this kind of thing fall under the same strict condemnation of God as any other law-breaker. There are no excuses for bullying, tale bearing, spreading of rumours, and engaging in malicious chin-wag! Bullies are expert at this! They can do it;

and they do it under the cover of showing concern and compassion and sympathy and understanding for the person they have targeted.

But look. What do we make of those who will stand idly by and do nothing about the bullying that is going on before their very eyes? What about *them*? What about those who are indifferent to the wrongdoing that is done in their name? They are also under the divine condemnation; there are no excuses and there are no exceptions.

Let me give you a couple of examples that will provide a window into this situation where ministers stand by, knowing that bullying abuse is going on in front of them, and do nothing. If you saw a man drowning, splashing about in a river and you had the means to rescue him, but you did not do it, would you be guilty of his death? Yes, you would. If you saw a fight on the street, and you refused to call the police, and someone was seriously injured, would you be guiltless? No, you would not. If you saw a house on fire and you refused to get help and phone for the fire brigade, could you live with yourself? Hardly.

Yet, the sad reality is that bullying goes on before the eyes of other ministers and elders, and they do nothing about it, simply nothing. They witnessed it and they may have been involved in it, maybe not actively. They were onlookers, they were bystanders, and they saw what other ministers were doing to a colleague, yet they did nothing to intervene or stop this cruelty. They are as despicable as those who do the actual bullying, just as those who provide a car, a safe house, work as a look-out, or dispose of incriminating clothing, etc, are as guilty as those who pulled the trigger or detonated the bomb. They had it in their power to intervene, and to step in, and save their colleague, but they refused to act.

What happens is that colleagues team up with the bullies; they take sides *against* their neighbour, the very behaviour that God through Moses condemns in v.16. They take sides with the bullies against the targeted person. I have seen that with my own eyes. Ministers whom I had considered friends and not just work colleagues, just sat silently and did nothing to intervene to stop the exploitation, the harassment, the manipulation, the bullying, the spiritual abuse. Nothing! Oh what great cowards these men were! What yellow bellies! What snowflakes! It is appalling, especially for those who are at the receiving end of it. Are they guiltless for what their colleagues did in their name to that minister or to any minister? Absolutely.

We have been stalked, as has another minister, stalked for weeks on end by a church elder, and that was horrendous. It was extremely unsettling, not least for the minister's wife. There was no point in wasting time in reporting this to the Presbytery, for its leaders just would not listen! This stalking was clearly visible, yet no one did anything to stop it. A church officer attacked physically a minister, yet the church authorities held the minister to be at fault. A church member accused another minister of sexual impropriety, but there was not a shred of evidence presented to back up the charge, and, thankfully, the authorities cleared him of any wrongdoing. Yet he felt forced out of the ministry. Yet the accusers go on as if nothing has happened. So do the bullies!

Domestic violence and abuse, child abuse, racial abuse; these are horrible cruelties. Yet, spiritual abuse in and by the church is ignored, covered up, and those guilty protected and promoted. You know, Agatha Christie could not have written this.

Yes, ministers bully each other, and that is a FACT! Sadly, no one will try to stop this evil cruelty in and by the church, no one. This spiritual abuse is on a par with these other forms of abuse. We must move to equate all forms of abuse, refuse to acknowledge any hierarchy of abuse, and not allow anything or anyone to distract us.

Why must this stop immediately? Why must the church repent of this now? Because, as God says through Moses, '*I am the LORD.*' That is why. There is no better reason or higher motivation to do so than this! He is saying, *'I am God, not you. I will call you to account on the last day and you will answer me with judgement-day honesty. There will be no hiding place for you, especially if you are a professing evangelical, and a man of the Word. Your condemnation will be all the more severe. You knew the truth, but you denied it. You lived in the light, but you snuffed it out. The greater the light and truth you had, the greater will be your responsibility before God on that last day. There will be no hiding place for you. You will call on the mountains and hills to fall upon you and hide you from the wrath of the Lamb on that Day,'* (*Revelation* 6:16)!

But today is the day of grace. I call on you to repent of your sin, and of the sins that drove you to this vile cruelty against your neighbour. Own up to Christ, confess it to Him, and admit that you have done these things. Admit the wrong you did, with others, to your brother. Come back to Christ. Seek His forgiveness, and know His cleansing.

Prayer:

O, LORD, as we come to you again today, we come in that Name that is above every other Name, the Name of Jesus. We come to You, LORD, because we can come to no other. You understand. You know what the victims and targets of bullying have been through, and are still going through to this day. You know the callousness, self-righteousness, and arrogance of the bullies who believe that it was right for them to do what they did.

LORD, have mercy on us all. We need Your mercy. We come to You. Forgive us, O God, for all the wrong we have done to our own lives, and to others. And help us, LORD, to follow You more closely in the days to come.

For it is in Jesus' precious Name that we pray. Amen.

6. Love Your Neighbour as Yourself!

Leviticus 19:17,18.

The sub-title that I have given to these studies is *Bullying and Spiritual Abuse*. This is our sixth study in this particular issue. I am very grateful for the feedback that has come, because if the church is bullying you, I can assure you, you are not the only one who is being bullied or spiritually abused in and by the church. There can be no doubt, surely in anyone's mind, that what drives bullying is heart hatred against your brother, the one whom you have targeted. If love is absent from your heart, then it is no wonder that your heart cannot tolerate that person. Also, your heart, just like nature, cannot tolerate a vacuum, so if love is absent from your heart, it will be replaced by hatred, the polar opposite of love. Heart hatred in the church is spiritually abusive.

The very thought of a brother being treated as a foe or as an enemy is repulsive to the Christian mind. Surely, you know that as well as I do. Indeed the blessing of almighty God is withheld because there is *'sin in the camp.' 'Sin separates you from your God.'* God sees and knows your heart far, far better than you know it yourself. It tells us that *'your iniquities have separated you from your God,'* (*Isaiah* 59:2).

And what is the result? He will 'not hear our prayers.' Maybe that is why you find that God is not hearing or answering your prayers! It is because there is sin in your heart, known sin, willing sin. That heart sin shows itself as hatred for your brother. Sin does not live outside the human heart. It is the disease of the soul. The effect of that abuse lasts a lifetime.

I met with three different ministers in the last five days. They are all suffering the ill effects of bullying and spiritual abuse. Each one of them, and others that I know, are suffering from lifelong health issues. The very churches in which they had given their lives to serve Christ and the Gospel battered them, bruised them, crushed and abused them. Yet, nobody seems to care. Why did the church do this, do you think?

As Moses tells us here in v.17, it is because of heart hatred in their abusers towards them. The biblical explanation is the one that we need to go back to and heed, and take to heart. Heart hatred has done this. You could not have abused another minister, another brother, another colleague, had you not had hatred in your heart towards him. Besides, that heart hatred towards another is the polar opposite of love for your neighbour. Where there is a total absence of true biblical love for your neighbour, you will always have bullying and spiritual abuse. That is the logical outcome. No amount of Bible words will ever convince a biblically informed mind otherwise.

I was speaking with a minister a few weeks ago. Bullies hounded him out of his church a few decades ago. When speaking to him, I saw something I had not seen for ages. It is probably 35 years since this happened to him. What did I see? I saw his lips trembling as he described how much that evil behaviour had damaged his health.

The last time I saw that was when I visited a former soldier whom IRA terrorists had traumatised. He told me he never opened the door to anyone. He invited me in and sat down. When he began to speak, I heard his dentures rattle in his mouth! He was beside himself. IRA death squads traumatised the *former soldier*, and church terrorists traumatised the *minister*. It was the same response in each case.

This is evidence of trauma brought about by bullying and spiritual abuse. There is only one word to describe this, and that is the word 'cruelty.' The brutal treatment that these good men received was evident and seen clearly. Bullying is cruel to an incalculable degree. And the only pond that this behaviour can come from is a heart that is filled with hatred, v.17.

God says through Moses that we are not to do that. There can be no doubt that such ministers who behave in that vile way do not believe the Bible, and that, despite all their religious words. They do not believe this basic overarching theme of the Bible concerning human relationships, *'Love your neighbour.'* They do not believe that! They do not believe the words of the Lord Jesus Christ or His apostles. It is that clear. What did Jesus say? He said *'you will know them by what they produce,'* (*Matthew* 7:15,16). If the tree produces cruel fruit, then it is a bad tree. Moreover, if the gardener does not prune that tree so that it can bear good fruit, he will gather it up and throw it into the fire. That pictures what will happen to those who produce rotten, poisonous, toxic, dangerous fruit.

What does John Calvin say? Every man's mind ought to be towards his neighbour, and this teaching could not be better expressed it many pages than in this one sentence, *'Love your neighbour.'* It seems that extreme Calvinists are the worst examples of the reformer's fine words. The more extreme they are, the less loving they turn out to be. Have you noticed that? What I would say to them is this: go and study what it means to *'love your neighbour,'* not just in words but in practical actions.

Earlier in *Genesis* 49, Moses equates wrath and bondage. Just as bondage is cruel, so also is bullying. David speaks of hatred being cruel, (*Psalm* 25:19). Here is what really hits the nail: Solomon says, '*the tender mercies of the wicked are cruel*' (*Proverbs* 12:10). That means that even when bullies speak kindly to you, what they say is like a knife into your heart. It is like salt into the wounds that they have inflicted. It stings. It hurts. The fire *still* burns!

Let me illustrate this. Reading a letter I got from a church officer about 30 years ago which was about all the things that I should not be doing and ends up 'wishing me every blessing for the future.' I found those words toxic and repulsive. That is what wicked people do, you see; that is how they live. They are cruel. What sound psychology this is! This cruelty comes out of their innermost being, out of their heart. All the issues of life come out of the heart, (*Matthew* 12:34,35; 15:18). When the heart is wrong with God, evil spills out and damages people. If that is not bullying and spiritual abuse, then I do not know what is! That psychology is good. Even someone who is wicked, somebody who has bullied and spiritually abused you, offers kind words, they are being cruel, deeply cruel.

However, hatred *per se* is not wrong; but we must only use it against evil, never against another person.

We must hate evil with all our heart, as the Bible teaches. But we are to love God with all our heart and we will love our neighbour with all our heart, too. These things are all connected. And *your brother is also your neighbour.* So many seem to forget that today. The apostle John writes, *'whoever hates his brother is a murderer,'* (*1 John* 3:15). Calvin adds that although there may be no outward signs of hatred, yet the internal feeling is accounted murder before God. Therefore, from the Apostle John's perspective, our spiritual abusers are murderers; they have murder in their hearts. They have death in their hearts towards the person that they have targeted. Furthermore, Jesus tells us that *'no murderer has eternal life in him.'* This is criminal.

Three realities motivate murder: power, greed (money), and sex. In the case of the bully church, it is usually the first two that predominate, but not exclusively. They have been given, or have taken to themselves, the power they use to destroy, or murder, another – the target. They use that power without any regard to the damage they leave behind.

On the greed motivation, the same applies. Jealousy and greed are often linked. If they think someone else is better at something than they are, they will do all they can to ensure that the other person, the target, is disadvantaged in every way possible. They want to get the preaching opportunities, and the money that accompanies these, so that they do the necessary to stop the other man. At the bottom of it all is this heart-hatred of the victim.

Bullying cannot occur where heart hatred is absent. Now, look at what Moses says here. If a neighbour, not a brother, needs rebuke, then do it positively, kindly, with grace, in understanding, and brotherly love.

Moreover, let the rebuker do it with a view to helping that individual, not condemning him. Let him do it with the idea of resolving whatever his issues are, not casting him down; and with the view of restoring that person to communion with God if that has been broken, and to communion with God's people. Do it openly, not secretly or behind his back, or even behind closed doors.

Nothing we do but has the thought of God is upon it. He has a word of condemnation or sanction respecting it. We all have to do with him, to whom we must give account one day. There will be no excuses. So be warned. Be warned how you treat the servant of Christ. Be warned how you deal with the Gospel man in your church.

V.18 goes on to tell us that we are to take no vengeance, nor are we to hold a grudge against the children of your people. God rules this out, too, outlawed by God himself, speaking through Moses. The problem is that bullies do not believe this. They will hammer ministers until their health is on the edge of total collapse.

Three men I met with in the last five days have had serious health problems ever since the bullying and spiritual abuse. I know these men. I have been there myself. Ministers having to undergo counselling for ages. I understand that. I had to go under psychiatric care for 18 long months, and was on the verge of being sectioned under the Mental Health Act for my own safety. That is how bad this can be. This is not fairy-tale stuff. This is the real world. This is what goes on within the churches. They beat you emotionally, mentally, and spiritually until they have defeated you. That is their intended goal from the beginning. They wanted to destroy you. And imagine if you can, the pleasure they felt when their target was destroyed to the point where they were no longer able to work. They thought they had done a great job. It was a job well done, in their minds. 'Let us get on with our own business again. Let us forget about that scoundrel.' How proud they would have been over there success. They beat that bad man into submission. That was their purpose, you see. They freed the Church of his malignant influence.

That has been a very dark, negative, and depressing picture, was it not? But thankfully God does not leave it there because through Moses He says, in effect, there at the end of v.18, *'Here is how you should live. Not in the way that I have described up until now. Here is how you ought to live. You are to love your neighbour as yourself. Instead of hatred in your heart towards your neighbour, I want you to have*

love in your heart towards him. Never do anything harmful to him but always seek to benefit him in any way you can."

You see, if love really governed all that you did, there would be no such thing as bullying and spiritual abuse in the church. But because bullying and spiritual abuse are there, this part of Scripture has not been obeyed. Clearly, that is the case. If God tells us to love our neighbour and to love our brother, why are we not doing that? Why do they not do that in a biblical manner? What is so disappointing is that those who shout about believing the whole Bible from *Genesis* to *Revelation*, those who claim it is infallible, inerrant, and the inspired Word of God; those who say that they are Bible men, expositors of Scripture who accept the supremacy of Scripture in the life of the church and the Christian, these are often the very people who inflict the deepest suffering on God's servants. You could not make it up, could you? You do not seek revenge on these people if you have suffered at their wicked hands. Leave it to God. You go on loving, for God is not mocked. He will repay. Just take a step back and leave it in God's hands. Hand them over to the loving God, for He will do a far better job than you or I could ever do. This is a time when we must trust Him. Cast your all on Him, and remember this: *you are not on your own.* I told you that in an earlier study. *You are not to blame for the bullying and spiritual abuse you suffered; the bully is!* No, *you are not on your own.* Knowing what they have put you through, it is the bully, the abuser, who is totally to blame for what has been done to you.

I am saying to you, that others know something of what you are going through. Contact me, if you wish. Do not allow this horrible experience to simmer in your soul and isolate you because that is the objective of their plan against you; to isolate you. How many of God's dear servants have been ghosted by serving ministers in the churches! They have been 'sent to Coventry.' They could not even look at them, speak to them, or say hello. What drives that rudeness is hatred in their hearts, nothing else! *You are not on your own.* The Lord will meet with you through other believers who understand. So, do not stay away. Do not isolate yourself. Do not cut yourself off. Whatever else you may do, that is the worst thing that you could do.

However, whatever you do, do not go to the very people who have inflicted this pain on you. Why do I say that? For this reason: they will re-traumatise you if you go to them. Do you remember what Solomon said in *Proverbs* 12:10? *'The tender mercies of the wicked are cruel.'* Do you know something else? Not only do they not care a toss about you, they do not even know how to help you, even if they wanted to, because they do not understand your position and condition, nor do they understand the basics of pastoral theology.

I say to you, in closing, stay clear of those people. You would never send an IRA terrorist to investigate the activities of his IRA colleagues and partners, would you? You would never get an honest report or outcome from such people. If your church has traumatised you, if your church has treated you cruelly, then whatever you do, do not go to them for help. They will retraumatise you and deal with you cruelly. Stay clear of them. That was the advice given to me by trauma experts during my work with the victims of terrorism. There are others who can and will help you; *you are not on your own.*

Prayer.

Father, we bow humbly before You, broken in heart and spirit. We come as those who have been cast to the very dust. We come to You as those who have been hounded, battered, bruised, and crushed; those who suffer from this every day since, and who will until the end of their lives.

Lord, give us grace, we pray. Pour out Your Spirit upon us, and fill our hearts with Your grace. Let us know Your mercy every day; and fill our hearts with love for You. Help us to have a loving disposition towards those who did such cruel wickedness.

We turn to You now. We give our lives afresh over to You. We hide in the Rock that is 'higher than I.' We come to You, Lord; shelter us, protect us, and build a hedge around us in these evil days, and keep us safe while these storms rage outside of us, but especially inside of us. They are in our minds morning, noon, and night. Our hearts are filled with the hurt and the damage that these evil people have inflicted on us.

So, Lord, we turn to You. We cast ourselves upon Your mercy. We surrender ourselves to Your purpose for our lives. Lord, help us to trust You as we walk through this 'valley of the shadow of death.' Help us, like David, to 'fear no evil.' Help us, like David, to know that You are with us.

Thank you that we are yours through the blood of the Cross, through faith in Christ. Help us, Lord, to walk accordingly, and to be strong and of good courage.

All of these things we ask in Jesus' Name. Amen.

7. Christian Love Removed!

1 Corinthians 1:1-3

Our last chapter dealt with the teaching of Moses, *'Love your neighbour as you love yourself.'* I continue our studies into this overall subject of *bullying and spiritual abuse*, and I want you to come with me as we study the same theme from the New Testament. Turn with me in your Bibles to *1 Corinthians* 13 and read the first three verses of this wonderful hymn of praise to love. Paul has been dealing with the gifts of the Spirit. He takes us to the very summit of what he was saying in chapter 12. God says that we are to *'love your neighbour as you love yourself.'* This great truth is writ large over the entire Bible. You cannot read any part of the Old or New Testaments without them confronting you with this precious truth. This is a necessary requirement of the Christian. It is to mark and characterise the true disciple. He is to wear it as the badge of his discipleship, the badge of love.

This gift or grace of love is the great antidote to sin amongst brethren and neighbours. If love dominated our lives, then hatred would be stone dead. No harm would ever be done to anyone if this were to be there, if this were to be observed, no question about that. There will be no wars, no family disputes, no marital breakdowns, no rapes, no thefts, no frauds, no murders, nothing like that. Sin would be gone, putting it at its lowest. Kindness, understanding, and compassion would be everywhere and would fill everything.

Now what is this love like? Theologians say that 'love' is the 'queen of all the graces.' It outshines all the others as the sun outshines the planets, as Thomas Watson (c.1620-1686), the English Puritan, said. This is the love with which God loved the world, *agape* love. Besides, that love still loves the world today. It is a special love. It is a typically godly love, and it is typically Christian love, a love that 'comes from the new birth,' as Iain H. Murray put it. He adds, 'Love is the consequence of the indwelling of God.' Where God dwells, there is love.

The opposite is also true, sadly. However, this is a divine love that always finds a way of overcoming whatever obstacles it faces. It always looks for a way to overcome in any and every situation. It is a love that gives to the ultimate point of sacrifice. And it can never be defeated! That is God's love, and it is real love.

Put simply, it is goodwill to those who do not deserve any good, but rather the opposite. It is 'sin-bearing love.' And why that kind of love? Because anything short of that would not achieve what God wanted to achieve, namely, the salvation of the world. Everything else was destined to fail. So *'love your neighbour.'* I know this is difficult. We are to love our neighbour, even if he is our enemy. We do it with a love that bears their sins, not in an atoning way. But it bears their sins in the sense that it does not allow them to become an obstacle to a relationship.

However, it is one thing to talk about love; how do you prove it? How do you show that love? How does anyone prove the reality of their love for another? Well, they do it by backing up what they say with the right action. When you say you love someone, you show it by your actions, by your behaviour, by what you do. That is just what God did. He took real and necessary action to show the height, depth, width, and the breadth of His love for the world. We, you and I, if we are Christians, no matter what our standing in the church might be, we are expected to do exactly the same.

Now how are you to show that love to your neighbour or brother? Well, you show by acting as God acted. We have a great Example here, a great Pattern that we can follow, and we are to imitate Him. We do it by acting as God acted. We do it by allowing nothing in the other person to put us off doing him good. You do it by allowing nothing to intervene, no obstacles, and no barriers. You do it by going *'the extra mile'* to help, support, and restore him. You do it by being a crutch for him at times when things are really tough, and they can be tough in the Christian life, and they can also be very tough for the minister. Do not think that when you see your minister walking into the pulpit on Sunday that everything for him is rosy. It is not! He is doing the work that he is there to do. He could be breaking up inside. He could be going through a dark valley. He could be at his wit's end. He might be at the end of his tether! You do not know that. Everyone finds it difficult at times. That is why Christian love is so utterly necessary. Besides, by love we overlook the weaknesses and the sins of that other person and we try to get them back on track again. What does God say through Moses? What does God's Son say? *'Love your neighbour.'*

When speaking with other ministers who have not been through the trauma of bullying and spiritual abuse, the unasked question could well be, 'And what kind of help do you think we could give?' I answered this unasked question to a former colleague a few months ago when I admitted that the one thing a bullied minister wants more than anything else at that time is for someone, a friendly colleague, just to put his arm around him, assure him that he is his friend, and show some semblance of care. The bullying's *modus operandi* is to achieve the isolation of the target/victim.

To ease this, one can make sure that the individual is not left isolated. He thinks that he is the only one to whom the church has done this, and that is scarily isolating. The church has done this to other ministers and Church leaders know that if they can effectively isolate the target and ensure, *by fair means or foul*, that his colleagues do not contact him, the broken minister will die a slow painful death.

I know that there are Christians who show a very strange kind of love to others. They will tell you and they will preach to you to show love to others, but their own expression of that love can be very different from what we read in Scripture. In fact, it is so strange that you could hardly call it 'love' at all.

When they resort to bullying and spiritual abuse to get their own way, then what are they doing? They are denying the Gospel and they are disobeying the oft-repeated Word of God on this matter. When you are dealing harshly with a brother or a neighbour, you are not fulfilling the law of Christ. That is the bottom line. They do not show that God-like love, that Calvary love, as they should. That is tragic and should cause us to blush every time this truth faces us. We fail so lamentably.

Now, there is a great hymn of praise to love in the New Testament in *1 Corinthians* 13. What a hymn this is! Inspired, inerrant, infallible, and preserved by God down through the centuries. How radical that love is, and how warm it is just to read those verses.

At the end of the previous chapter, Paul urged the Corinthians to desire the best spiritual gifts for the glory of God. And no gift is so useful and glorifying to God than love, love to God and love to others. It is the 'queen of the graces.' If you excel in love, you are at the very pinnacle of the Christian life. If you excel in showing love to God and your neighbour, you are at the very summit of true religion. That is where we want to get to, is it not? Right to the summit.

Now, love is easier talked about than shown? We all know that. But those who talk most about love do not always show it, do they? One of the old writers, John Boys, said, 'He loves but little, who tells how much he loves.' That is so true, especially of the theological liberals. They are the people who seem to have hijacked *love*, and then imposed that distorted version on others, but they are not very good at it themselves, are they? Yes, they are big into the huggy, lovey-dovey, sloppy kind of love. You know the brigade I am talking about; mere sentimentalism.

They talk about love more than they show it. That is not *agape* love.

However, evangelicals are no better. They fail lamentably there too, and I am thinking about ourselves. We may have all our theology spot on, we may know all our doctrines, and we may claim to be Bible men. Yet when it comes to showing love, especially when it is needed most, you could not see them for the dust. They disappeared and seemed to have been spirited away, invisible. Indeed, when opportunity came to show that basic love, or even basic good manners, that, too, just seemed to have evaporated.

I could tell you stories of that from my own experience and from the experience of brother ministers who saw this with their own eyes. Invisible love is no love at all. I want us to dwell right here, for in the first three verses of this chapter, Paul tells us some quite amazing things about the necessity and the importance of love. He says, 'Even though I might be able to speak with human and angelic tongues; I may be the best speaker in the world, and be the best orator that ever entered a pulpit. I might be a great conference speaker, a speaker at Bible conventions. However, if I have no love, what am I? I am no better than sounding brass, or a clanging cymbal.' That is it! What does that mean? It means that all your fine words are nothing but verbal noise.

They are empty. They are meaningless. Hollow. Insincere. Futile. You could add the adjectives to that list. 'Oh, I'm a great evangelical minister. I am a Gospel preacher. I am reformed. I believe the Bible from cover to cover; every jot and tittle of it, I believe, is inspired, infallible, is inerrant, and is breathed out by God.'

However, if you have no love, this is just hot air. What does that mean? It means there is nothing in it. All your fine sounding words, they are just a lot of noise. They are like crashing metal. It's all talk. A religion of words only, there is nothing behind it. The man who is absorbed with saying rather than doing has become nothing more than sound, or noise. That is it. What has that brought you to? It has brought you to *nothing* and has left you there. Do you see all your tongue speaking and miracle working; put them into their proper place. They are nothing beside love. Do not elevate them to the highest position for they are not to be there. Put love for God and love for your fellow man at the very top. Desire that above all else, for that is the summit, that is the pinnacle of Christian experience. It is the most important thing of all.

For truth to be genuine, appropriate action must back it up, not harmful, hurtful, or damaging action. That is the very negation of that about which I am talking. It is not appropriate action. How does anyone know you love him? By your actions. We show we love them by what we do. Words of love backed up with loving actions is what is required here. That is what Paul has been calling for, and that is what Jesus taught before Paul's time. There is no point in being well educated, having a degree, being knowledgeable about prophecy, and understand all the mysteries of revelation, and even have a faith that could remove mountains, but have no love; it comes to zero.

You see, it is love that gives substance to all your other achievements, is it not? Even if you give your body as a martyr to the flames and you do it without love, there is no profit there for anyone, least of all yourself. It is a waste of time, it is a waste of energy, and ultimately it is a waste of a life. There is no benefit for anyone for it is all a show, it is just irritating noise, religious words, great words, perhaps, but just words and no more.

Now, the same applies to those with great spiritual gifts and knowledge in the church. What may we expect of them? Not holy behaviour in many cases, that is one thing for sure. Because, like the Pharisees that we spoke about in earlier sermons, these men are graceless. In fact, they show the very opposite of love for God's people. Where love is absent, no behaviour of any kind, no matter how depraved or wicked it might be, can be ruled out. A man may have many gifts from God that he uses well, but if he does not have love, those gifts cannot stop him being nothing but a dead instrument. All his gifts, all his talents would be without any value whatever. I may be great in the eyes of others, but in God's eyes, I am *nothing*. As Charles Hodge put it, love is superior to all spiritual gifts, and, I might add, abilities. Love is better than tongues, better than prophecies, better than knowledge, better than miracles, better than being charitable, better than being a martyr.

Paul says to us, through this letter to the Corinthians, *pursue love,* (*1 Corinthians* 14:1). Pursue it, brothers and sisters. In all your dealings with others, let love be shown. Let love for your brother man shine brightly. Let it rule every decision and every action that you take. In every situation of difficulty, let love reign. Do the loving thing. Now, when love is absent, bullying and spiritual abuse will result and be present and active. I have seen this with my own eyes, and others have seen the same. However, when love is present, when love is predominant, then bullying and spiritual abuse are totally impossible.

Ministers and church members have known destruction because the church has denied love to them. Yes, denied, withheld love from them. No man of love will ever harm another, because kindness will be evident. Where there is true love, there will be humility, modesty, and unselfishness. They will always seek the other person's well-being, and be in the pursuit of goodness, not badness. We must all assess ourselves against this standard, must we not?

Let me ask you, 'How are *you* doing at the moment? If the Lord Jesus Christ was to write a letter to you or to your church, what would He say in it? Would He be complementary? Or, would He be condemnatory? What would He say about *you*? What would He say about *your church*? Would He condemn *your church*? Would He condemn *you*?

This applies also to the victims of bullying and spiritual abuse. How are you handling this situation, my brother victim? At the end of the day, you see, it is love alone that counts. When you strip everything else away, love alone counts. Leave this out, and you have *nothing*. You may have made decisions, you may have taken actions, but God counts those decisions and actions illegitimate, and unjust, and wicked, and wrong, because it is love alone that counts and triumphs ultimately. Forget about your orthodoxy, and forget about your confessional correctness; for these amount to *absolutely nothing* if love is absent.

Prayer:

Father, we bow before You after listening to Your Word coming to us. Lord, Your Word has gone like a dagger into our hearts. We admit our failures. Lord, we have not done what You want us to do. We have sinned against You, and that is much worse than failure. Come to us today. Lord, be gracious to us. Show us Your mercy, we pray. Help us, by Your grace, to attend seriously to these words that we have read. Grant, Lord, that we will seek to work these out in our lives and in our interactions with others. Thank You that we can turn to You. Thank You for Your love for us, a love that is unconquerable.

We come back to You again, the God of Calvary, the God whose wrath was shown at Calvary, but also His love that was to hide our sins and guilt from Your sight. Thank You for Your love for us, a love that is unconquerable. Help us to stay there, Lord, and then to go out from the Cross to serve You. We ask all these things in Jesus' Name. Amen.

8. By Their Fruits!

1 Corinthians 1:4-8a

The subject is bullying and spiritual abuse, and the focus is, of course, on bullying and spiritual abuse within the Church of Jesus Christ. These sermons have shown the very great difference there is between those who believe the Bible and those who use bullying and spiritual abuse as a management tool to get their way. Before we proceed, please read *1 Corinthians* 13:4-8a.

Now, our Lord Jesus Christ spoke some very challenging words to His disciples. Besides, we find one of those very challenging words that He spoke to His disciples in *John* 13:35. *'By this will all men know that you are My disciples, if you have love for one another.'* Now you would think that that would be unnecessary to say to disciples of Jesus, but obviously, it is not. Obviously, they fall far short of what Jesus wants for His own people, a truth that they often hide behind to get away with deliberate wickedness. In addition, this love that Jesus speaks about is the believer's badge of membership in His Kingdom. How do you know if someone is a Christian, a follower of Jesus? You will know if love flows from his life.

I remember hearing something that John Wesley, the

Methodist leader of the mid-1700s, said in answer to a question as to whether or not Mr So and So was a Christian, naming him. Wesley said, *'I don't know. I don't live with him.'* That is a very sharp statement, is it not? What a man is to the outside world may be very different from what he is 'behind closed doors.' How lovely it would be if what we were in the public was exactly the same in the privacy of our own homes, and also in the closed meetings where a colleague's future ministry is being discussed and decided upon!

How great it would be if we could say the same about what happens in our churches. They appear to be all smiles and pleasant and nice on the outside and in public, but that is not always how they are 'behind closed doors.' Are they always pleasant, full of grace? Compassionate? Understanding? Jesus says, *'By this will all men know that you are My disciples, if you love one another.'*

Now, sadly, this is missing from the church when she degenerates into a mere religious institution. I have heard it said, 'There's no grace in law.' That is so true. Either you are keeping the law, abiding by the law, or you are not. There is no in between. There is no greater error than when the church places more faith on keeping church law, than on extending grace and love;/ then you have a serious problem. What is that problem? It is bullying, spiritual abuse within the body of Christ. These happen where love is not present. Where love suffused the whole fellowship, you will never find bullying and spiritual abuse. What a blessing it would be where bullying and spiritual abuse are as far from the church as the east is from the west! That is what we want, is it not? Is not that what Jesus wants for His Body, His Bride? Nothing there to spoil her beauty, nothing there to taint her. That is what He wants.

But sadly, and you know this as well as I do, that is not the case. Why? Because of the absence of true Christian love in the hearts of God's people, Christ's disciples, God's ministers. They may talk about it, they may even preach about it, but when hardy comes to hardy, it is very thin on the ground. It just is not there, in fact. Even those who want to show love to a targeted minister, cannot do so because there would be serious repercussions for his own ministerial career, and protecting his career at all costs is what drives him. When love has gone or been driven out of the church, anything goes. You can treat others any way you like. You can be as violent as you like with God's servants as one minister found to his great cost. An office bearer physically assaulted him, yet his oversight found him at fault. It happened in this country, a few months ago (2022).

Some years ago, a group of church members accused their minister of sexual abuse. Yet, following intense Presbytery and police investigations, they cleared him of all wrongdoing. Yet because of the effect of *'mobbing'* within his church, he and his family felt forced to flee from Northern Ireland and go and work in a foreign land. This is happening in the church today. What is it? It is bullying and spiritual abuse.

Now, some churches even get rid of a minister without bringing any charges against him whatever. They seem to rule the church by whims. This man was guilty of nothing but spoiling the ecumenical hobby horsing of the liberals and depriving them of their free jaunts all over the world. Barefaced vindictiveness was apparent. And what is that? That is bullying and spiritual abuse.

Nevertheless, these things only happen when the church has driven love out of her. These awful experiences carry with them lifelong trauma for those who have been affected by them! Men never really get over the negative effects and the impact of bullying on their lives; nor do their wives and families. They will take that hurt with them to the grave.

I know it can be somewhat idealistic to imagine that churches can learn from their mistakes, because as the philosopher Hegel said, 'history teaches us that history teaches us nothing.' We just do not learn from our past mistakes. The churches are very slow learners, because they are convinced of their own infallibility. However, that does not mean that Scripture has no teaching for us as we seek to live for Christ in this sinful world. Here in *1 Corinthians* 13, we have an entirely divinely inspired hymn, dedicated to dealing with these very matters. Now, why do you think Paul wrote this hymn in chapter 13? Was it not because he knew that there was lovelessness going on within the Corinthian church, despite her obvious spirituality? Was it because he knew that members were up to no good? Were there all kinds of rascality going on within and by the church, maybe even by the leaders? So Paul felt compelled, under the influence of God's Spirit, to write this letter setting out what true Christian love really is.

Remember, Paul wrote this letter to the church in Corinth; and Corinth was a Greek city that was associated with all kinds of sexually immoral behaviour. They were just like Sodom and Gomorrah in the Old Testament. To call anybody a Corinthian was to be a fornicator. If someone called a young woman a Corinthian girl, she was a prostitute. This was an openly immoral city, and, to the people there, love meant only one thing - sexual perversity. It was the most morally corrupt city in the ancient world.

So just imagine for a moment or two the impact that the Apostle Paul's epistle had when it was first read in the city church! He was promoting an understanding of love that was foreign to what they understood love to be. I am sure there were people there in that church who just did not like it, and who wondered what Paul was talking about when he was setting forth true love?

In Corinth, you see, love was all about getting for yourself, not about giving, as Christian love is! *'For God so loved the world that He gave'* (*John* 3:16). His love was not about getting. He *gave*. But in Corinth, you see, it was all about *getting* for yourself, *getting* pleasure, *getting* excitement, losing control of yourself in some kind of sexual orgy. There was no kindness whatever in Corinthian love. In Corinth, they drove man after woman and woman after man, and sometimes after their own sex. They had to have *that* person before someone else gets them. In Corinth, you had to parade yourself so that those whom you want to attract actually see you and want you for themselves. You just have to stand out from the crowd, in the wrong sense, and so make yourself different. You had to make yourself appealing, tempting, alluring. And you do that through dress, or the lack of it. That was Corinth. The whole emphasis was on being suggestive, enticing, and seductive. That is how they viewed love. It was all about *getting* for yourself.

You know, take the sexual connotation out of it, and is not that what worldly love in the church looks like today? It is about me proving myself right. It is about me exercising the power that I have for *my* good, so that others will look upon me and say, 'Isn't he a great man.' So different from the love the Paul goes on to expound here in this letter.

What he exposed in this letter, was so different from what was 'the done thing' in Corinth in the fir+st century. For Paul, love is not something that is puffed up with its own self-importance or self-image. In other words, in Christian love, there is no pride to be seen anywhere. Pride was evident in Corinthian culture and life, you see.

In addition, being *'puffed up'* with pride meant that they opposed those who did not join with them in their hypocrisy. That is where pride comes in. I have seen that on the streets of this country, in Belfast and in Londonderry where we stood preaching the Gospel, and yet we were harangued, shouted at, even things thrown at us because we were 'different' from the crowd that was there. That is what those who lacked love are saying to us. 'You are not one of us and you do not belong to us. You have no right to be here.'

However, v.4 teaches us something totally different from that. Look at Paul's description of true love as being wholesome and pure. True love is patient and kind. When my case came before the church's Supreme Court in September 1992, it gave me five months to seek reconciliation with the other elders. The following March (1993), the Judicial Commission decided to loose me from my pastoral charge. A former clerk of the General Assembly stated to the General Assembly in June 1993 that it had speeded through my case with indecent haste.

What does Paul say? He says that love, true love, is patient. Yet, these people who were dealing with my case, wanted to get through it as quickly as possible, and what that former clerk was actually admitting was that biblical love was not in evidence in their dealings with me. The patience that characterises Christian love was wholly absent from that ecclesiastical court.

Now, what an admission that was from that former clerk. Yet the General Assembly completely and utterly ignored what he confessed. True love has an infinite capacity for endurance. It keeps on doing what is right, despite the circumstances and despite any pressure that may come from other ministers, and despite opposition to do what is right. It does not give up on a person and it does not give up easily, does it? Love perseveres until it reaches a good outcome. It points to patience with people. Love does not look for speedy solutions to difficulties, as was done in my situation. It shows outstanding kindness to others. Whatever is thrown at it, love responds with goodness towards those who mistreat it. Love always gives itself to those who need support and who need it every step of the way. Love never gives up. Loving people go in service to others, of their neighbour, and of one another. In this way, *'all men will know that you are My disciples, if you have love for one another.'* Therefore, love for one another is what Jesus says, but what does the church give? It gives damage, destruction, hurt, rejection.

Why this rejection of the doctrine of love? Why is the biblical teaching of love so despised by those who think they are right? Well, I can give one simple answer to that question, and that is the reaction to the perversion of love as expounded by the theological liberals. Theirs was a namby, pamby kind of love. Theirs was a love that did not have any content. It was sloppiness and softness dressed up in religious language, and without backbone to do the right thing. Put simply, it is ugly, illogical liberal love that is not Christian love. And it was to this caricature of true Christian love that many good men reacted. Moreover, with that reaction came the throwing out the baby with the bathwater. They over-reacted; they did not know how to deal with it. They went way overboard, and virtually denied that love was essential to Christian living. Thus, when evangelicals were in position where they could show love, they failed miserably. How sad that was!

What an indictment that is on the Church of Jesus Christ? Nobody knew what to do to do the loving thing, and nobody knew how to respond to difficult situations in a loving Christian manner. These were men of years of pastoral experience! They were far out of their depth and yet the church promoted these men to senior positions. It is the old Peter Principle all over again. They 'rose or were promoted to the level of their incompetence.' They overreacted by becoming extreme.

Just let me remind you again what Paul wrote there in verses 4 to 8. He said *'love suffers long, and is kind; love does not envy. Love does not parade itself, is not puffed up, does not behave rudely, does not seek its own, is not provoked, thinks no evil, does not rejoice in iniquity, but rejoices in the truth. It believes all things, hopes all things, endures all things.'* This passage ends up with these words: *'Love never fails or falls.'*

You see, there is no envy in love. There is no greed, spite, or bitterness in love. What is the limit of your love for your brothers and sisters in Christ? How far will you go to show them that love of which Paul speaks here? Is it true to say of you, as a seriously damaged minister told me, that your love 'will only stretch as far as your comfort will allow'? When your comfort is under pressure, do you pull back in order to keep in with the 'ruling class'? Is that how you operate your ministry? Do you join the 'don't knows' or 'did not see or hear anything' crowd? Is that where you are hiding? Do you watch how your decisions might affect your church career, your happiness and comfort? How are you matching up to these love qualities that Paul gives us here in this chapter?

Can you see yourself in what Paul writes? Is he talking about you? How far short do you fall in the light of these verses? Indeed, how far short we all fall in the light of these verses! We are failures, are we not? These verses that Paul writes here should actually convict us of our inner unrighteousness. They should show us something of our wicked hearts. Moreover, they should drive us immediately to the Cross to beg God's forgiveness and mercy. And those who come to Him, He will not drive away (*John* 6:37). They will be welcomed back into fellowship with Him.

I use that idea for this reason, that no man, but no man, will deliberately hurt or damage or seek to destroy another man, if the first man is living in fellowship with Christ. Did you get that? No one in the church, no minister, no elder, who knows the *new birth* will ever do anything to hurt or to destroy or to damage another man if he is living in fellowship with Christ? The only person who can damage and hurt another person is the one who is not living in communion with the risen Lord. That is challenging, is it not?

What about your everyday relationships with other people. Are there people you snub? Are there people from whom you turn away? Do you 'ghost' certain other people? Do you ignore them? Are there people you slight? That is very hurtful.

However, if you are truly living in communion with the risen Lord, you will not do that. You will come back to the Cross, back to Jesus as He died there for your sins, and beg God's mercy and forgiveness for your soul. Love never falls. It is always at its post. It is always in position, always at attention, always ready to serve.

Prayer:

Lord, You have come close to us again in this message through Your Word. You have put Your finger on sins in our lives, that we must deal with before You. We must come, O God, with deep and costly repentance, and with a repentance that will deal a death blow to our pride, our self-righteousness, and our arrogance, so that we can be restored to fellowship with you once more. Lord, be with us. Lord, show us that mercy. Show us the compassion that we failed or refused to show to our brother. Lord, come to us; bring us back, and, with Your help, we will never do that again. In fact, we will take every step we can to remedy the damage that we have done to Your servants.

Bless us, O God. Write your Word deep upon our hearts. Keep us close to You, O God, and bless our lives with Your presence.

For it is in Jesus' Name that we pray. Amen.

9. Their True Character Exposed!

1 Corinthians 13:4-8a

Now, if one thing is abundantly clear, it is this: that anyone who believes *1 Corinthians* 13 and other similar verses that teach a similar message will never be involved in bullying and spiritual abuse in the church. Period. This passage rules out such behaviour completely, everything that does not exhibit Christian love.

You might ask, 'Why is bullying and spiritual abuse so prevalent in the churches today?' That is a very good question. Let me give you one answer. The churches who use bullying and spiritual abuse as a management tool have torn *1 Corinthians* 13 out of their Bibles, it would appear, and all other teaching on the same subject. They do that because they no longer believe such teaching, nor do they now believe what our Lord Jesus Christ said on several occasions, namely, that you should *'love your neighbour as yourself.'* That simply does not come into it, even John's teaching on love. *'By this all men will know that you are my disciples, if you have love one to another,'* (*John* 13:35). The churches seem to have put a line through such verses with a red pen, and they no longer believe them; and through 'nods and winks,' have discouraged their members to live by these truths. That is a very serious thing to do. Verses like these call on Christians to love others, something I think we know and believe. Now, this never appears on the radar of many churches. It is all 'off-screen' stuff. In fact, bullying and spiritual abuse does not exist in the churches. At least that is what they tell us.

It is interesting and saddening, is it not, that senior churchmen do that kind of thing. They do not acknowledge that bullying and spiritual abuse go on in their religious organisation. Any problems that a minister runs into are automatically his own fault. 'He has brought this all on himself. Had he worked the way *we* worked, he would not experience this. *We* are perfect ministers, you see. We never had any serious problems in the church, but the victim must have done something way out of line that has brought this on himself. It is all his own fault, you see.'

There is a total denial about anything like this going on within the church. In fact, there are no bullies in the church; therefore, *we* cannot blame them for our problems. That is so logical, is it not? You cannot blame what does not exist! That is their argument. They stand aloof, washing their hands, Pilate-like, off all that has been done, either done by them or in their name.

Now, here is the point. If they are preaching the same message and insisting on the same biblical standard, as the victims of bullying do, then they, too, would be hounded like the others.

So what keeps them in their position? Let us assume that they do preach the same message, and they work to the same biblical standards as you. What is it that keeps them in their position? Well, one thing comes immediately to mind - *protectionism*. They have a shield around them that others do not have. They are a protected species, shielded, and defended. There are undercurrents that serve to protect certain ministers that do not protect other ministers. Oh, we are getting into the *deep church* here. We are *deep* into the inner workings of the church and into the very bowels of the church, into those *dark places* where only the initiated can enter.

You know, if you live in Northern Ireland, how the IRA and Mafia-type criminals can be and are protected by police and by the courts because they are 'inside.' Certain ministers have that same protection. They are untouchable. They can do whatever they wish and the church authorities will never touch them. They have a 'ring of steel' around them. They can run down their congregations to such a degree that their churches face closure because they become a financial liability to the denomination; but they are never touched! Why?

The establishment protects them. There is a 'ring of steel' around these men.

On the other hand, a minister can exercise a faithful Gospel ministry, have the support of the people, attendance at church services good, and giving good. What happens to him? The bullies throw him out of their ministry with utmost brutality and with a *smugness* that is sickening. You just have to listen to how they talk about their colleagues to grasp what is going on. These 'executioners' think themselves great men of God, great servants of the church, great men of the Bible. You know, it is not until a man becomes a soldier, that he knows what war is like. Only then does he know the cost that war exacts on him. This is like the man on the front line, facing the enemies of Christ and of the Kingdom of God. They know what it is like. There are men with the scars of fierce and bloody battle engrained on their very souls and bodies, scars that these men will take to their graves.

Armchair ministers know nothing of this, nor do committee-attending ministers know anything of the reality of spiritual battle. Ecclesiastical politicians get away with murder. Career ministers do not know anything of this. They have never been in the trenches of fierce spiritual battle.

Let me give you an example. I knew policemen who were stationed in barracks that sat right on or close to the border with our nearest international neighbour, the Republic of Ireland, the country that provided a safe haven for IRA terrorists when they committed their evil deeds of murder in my country. These men were stationed in those border towns in times of the greatest danger, and they could not wait to get moved out of those stations to somewhere safe.

I knew ministers who would not go to a border church. Why? Because that might not progress their ministerial career. It might not be safe for them or, they may get killed and maybe intimidated, maybe injured. You never see such men in the frontline trenches fighting the enemy.

Where there is love for Christ and the Gospel, you would go through anything and go anywhere to serve Him. Where there is love for the people of God, you will pay whatever price is necessary for you to be faithful to them. Where there is love, you will be faithful in all things, in all decisions that you take, and in everything that you do. Why? Because you have love in your heart for them. What is love, and why is love the determining force in your heart and life? Because the Lord Jesus Christ first loved you (1 John 4:19). That is the reason for being in the ministry. You are there because you love Jesus first and foremost.

So why do some ministers show no love to their colleagues when times are difficult? There is only one reason. They just have no love to give. Their love tank is empty. Love does not fill their hearts. Your erstwhile friends dropped you when the church dropped you. Why do you think that was the case? *First*, because they believed implicitly in the infallibility of the church, so when the church drops a minister, it is equal to God dropping him. *Secondly*, because they never were friends in the first place. There was no real love between the two of you. They used you to further their own ministerial careers. They were in it for a job, a nice, comfortable, well-paid job with great retirement benefits.

You see, true love never fails or falls, v.8a. False love does! It never stands. It cannot stand! It is just like prophecies – they will fail, tongues will cease, and knowledge will vanish away, v.8; but love never fails or falls. Just like these ministers, they are never there when you needed them most. They were temporary friends, just like the gifts. In fact, they were not friends, but mere work colleagues. That is why I do not want any of them at my funeral. Why would they come then? They did not come when I would have needed them. So why come then? Just to show face. They were not there for me when I needed them most, when my heart was breaking and crying out for someone to be a friend, and they were not there! Well, do not come because I do not want you there! They would not be there to comfort or to console, because the words of the wicked are cruel. They have no comfort to give. Why? Because they never knew the comfort of Christ in their own lives. That is what lies at the bottom of Paul's words here, is it not? But what are such ministers really like? They are ministers who lack *agape* love. What is more, in that lack of *agape* love, they leave behind very deep and pervasive scars in those they targeted for 'the treatment.'

I wonder, did these men have a difficult upbringing? Is that why they behave as they do against their colleagues? Did they have a hurtful childhood and adolescent experience and did that condition them into believing that this is what life is like - hard and difficult.

That is one explanation, but it is too Freudian to be biblical, though it is not without its merits. If 'hard and difficult' is the norm, then ministers must be dealt with in a 'hard and difficult' manner.

However, there is another explanation for that behaviour, the real explanation, and it is this. They behave as they do because of unconfessed and unresolved sin in their hearts. *Not only are they living in sin, but sin is living in them.* If they were living in holiness, they would never stoop to such depths of depravity, would they? If they were living in on-going, every day fellowship with Christ, they would never do such a thing. Only the man who is out of fellowship with the Saviour can behave in such a depraved way. The reality is that these men are not living in daily communion with Christ. Jonathan Edwards (1703-1758) hit the nail on the head when he said that the reason sin is not seen in all its ugliness is because the beauty of holiness is not acknowledged or appreciated.

Bullies are people who are self-centred, are they not? For them, it is *all about me*. Everything revolves around them. They must be the centre of everything, which is an undeniable trait of narcissism. Besides, that self-centredness leads them to loathe those who do not think similarly of them. If I do not think that these men are at the very pinnacle of church life, that they are so important, that they are the king-pin of everything that happens, then I will be despised. You can see that working out in church life, and indeed in everyday life, can you not?   The more engrossed they are with themselves, the more they despise others who are not also engrossed with them.

Their overall aim is to control these people, those whom they see as being 'under them.' While, on paper, they would not claim seniority over others in the church, they act as if they were the Pope of the church! To these men, 'attack is the best form of defence' against those whom they perceive as a threat to them. They are often envious of those perceived to be better than they are, since this serves to remind them of what is missing in their own lives. We will come to that in the next chapter. And they resent that, don't they? They are perfect, you see. They get on well. They are everything a minister should be, a model minister and pastor. But they cannot ever say that they are not responsible for ill-treating others because of the way they were brought up or the bad experiences that they had had. These contribute to who they are and how they act, but we must never use them as an excuse for their wrong behaviour. Nor can they hide behind bad church law as a defence for doing what they did. Even if the law is fine, the danger of misinterpreting it is always present, and very often misinterpretation of church law causes the deepest distress, hurt, and damage. If they show lack of love to others, then under God and in the eyes of Christ, they are responsible.

Bullies often exhibit a Jekyll and Hyde persona, do they not? In private and behind closed doors where there are no 'dangerous witnesses,' they can be vicious, intimidating, malicious, spiteful, yes, and threatening; they use threatening language to ministers. They appear to be all 'sweetness and light' in the public arena, and innocence personified. The bully, then, gives the impression that he knows of no other way of behaving. He will not accept that there are other and better ways of acting. This is not on the sheet for him. Now, what is all this but the very opposite of what Paul teaches us in *1 Corinthians* 13!

So, as I bring this chapter to a close, I do not want to

do so on a negative note. I want to close on a positive note. What must these men do? Well, the call of the Gospel is clear, is it not? They must repent of their sins of behaving in a loveless manner toward their colleagues, their brothers in Christ. Moreover, they must repent of their sin, the sin that lurks and dwells in their hearts. They must repent of letting the Lord Jesus Christ down in the most sacred office in the world, the Christian ministry. They must repent for bringing the Church of Jesus Christ into disrepute and causing God's blessing to be withheld from His people. They have acted wickedly and deliberately. The *only* thing they can do today is to repent, to fall down on their faces before the risen Christ and tell Him that they are sorry for their sinful behaviour, and ask for his forgiveness, promising never to do that ever again.

With these words of challenge, let us turn to God in prayer.

Prayer:

Lord, again today You have ploughed up our souls by Your Word and by Your Spirit. You have churned us up inside, oh God; You have told us things that we would prefer not to hear. You have helped us to see behind the curtain of what goes on in religious organisations and churches; and Lord, what we saw is not pleasant.

Father, we pray that You will touch the hearts of those who have been engaged in this sinful behaviour. Bring them to beg for Your mercy and forgiveness, and when they do repent, assure them of Your love and Your grace, and that You will restore them to usefulness within the people of God.

So, Lord, be with us. Bless us and keep us ever close to Yourself. In Jesus' Name we pray. Amen.

10. Defining the Bully!

1 Corinthians 13:4-8a

Now during my academic research into this subject of workplace bullying, I used a book by Dr Tim Field[3] on this particular subject. Tim spoke at a conference in Belfast and we worked on this particular evil, he doing radio interviews on workplace bullying in GB and I doing interviews in Northern Ireland. In his book, *Bully in Sight*, he catalogues, among other things, the following insights into the bully's general characteristics, the kind of a person he or she really is. Now, he could have written much of this by simply negating *1 Corinthians* 13, because how the bully lives, how he behaves, is the very antithesis of *1 Corinthians* 13.

Let me share with you some of Tim's findings. Here is what he says. The bully sees himself as a leader who is interested only in himself. He is a greedy, selfish individual who is not people orientated, and is usually insensitive and uncaring. He is someone who is unable to value what is good about someone, and is untrustworthy. He has at least two faces - one former colleague of mine described a minister who was dealing with him as having more faces than Big Ben. Therefore, he is at least two-faced. He is

---

[3] Field, T. *Bully in Sight.* (Oxfordshire: Wessex Press, 1996).

inconsistent, lacks conscience, and is insecure within himself, superficial, cowardly, and indeed a 'taker' rather than a 'giver,' someone who is out for himself. He is dictatorial, dominant, a hard-nosed kind of individual. He is power-orientated and vicious. He is vindictive, spiteful, critical, sarcastic, and uses guilt openly. He is someone who moves the goal posts to suit his own agenda, something that I found in my own experience, and it is horrible. He is a short-term thinker who is always looking for the quick fix to a serious situation (again, my experience). He is big into misrepresentation, and needs to assert his authority. He is usually a rigid and spineless individual who likes to trivialise the things that are going on.

The last thing that Tim Field mentions is that he is unwilling to apologise for wrong done. Now, if you compare this list of characteristics of the bully[4] with *1 Corinthians* 13, you will see where I am coming from. The bully is all that *1 Corinthians* 13 is not.

Now these typical bully characteristics recur with regular monotony. Identifying the essential traits of the bullying personality is not difficult, therefore, and the qualities that they exhibit are 'in your face' realities. Bullies are just wicked people.

---

[4] Field, 53-78. See also my unpublished M.Ed. dissertation, Ulster University, 1996.

Moreover, since the churches not only tolerate but also protect and promote such people, what is that saying about them? Or to put it a little bit more charitably, what about these men who are walking about the church acting as bullies, maybe onlookers knowing what's happening but doing nothing about it? Well, at rock bottom they are men who, like Peter, are following the Lord at a distance. They need to repent forthwith. And when they do repent and they realise that what they did was horribly wrong, they must then do everything in their power to make reparations to those that they have damaged. That will mean changes to church law and procedures, ensuring that the church removes those identified as bullies, and bringing former colleagues in from the cold and using them again in the service of the Gospel. Certainly, far too many bullying ministers view church law as the law of the Medes and the Persians that cannot be altered. These wicked people litter the churches today with those they set out to destroy, wreaking havoc wherever they operate.

Now, tell me, can you see any resemblance to *1 Corinthians* 13 in the behaviour of bullies? The love that Paul expounds in these verses is the polar opposite of how bullies operate in the churches. When Paul talks about love being patient and kind, v.4, where do we see these graces when the church courts deal with these difficult situations? Kindness is the last thing that we see in those situations. There is more likely to be shouting and threats than kindness and patience. Yes, these men can be harsh and very severe and utterly unforgiving because they think they are right. They have the power and they know it. This happens.

Senior ministers losing it when faced with a situation in which they know the minister is in the right, yet, out of fear, they do not support him. That is bizarre, is it not? That is v.5 of what Paul tells us here put extremely accurately in negative terms. Perhaps that verse or these verses are not even in the bully's Bible for all I know; if they even read their Bibles.

However, rudeness is the currency in which church business is often done when a minister is brought before the courts. Now when a minister resorts to parading his own authority, exalting himself as the fount of all knowledge, and daring anyone, in fact, to differ from him, declaring that his interpretation alone is right, and the minister has no right to differ from him, then you see a very different character to the smiley, pleasant, and nice one that portrays himself in public. Does that display *1 Corinthians* 13?

When these men go too far to get their own way, imagining that to be God's way, they are seeking their own, v.5, something that true love never does. They are seeking their own, without a doubt. It is their way or the highway. Indeed, from the outset, those hearing cases already have their minds made up, as to the outcome, and in this way they are thinking evil of the minister under investigation, v.5, and in whose case they are to judge righteous judgement. Indeed the entire investigation process is a sham. It is the perversion of justice; and how many dear servants of Christ have been put through this mincer, only to come out battered and bruised almost beyond recognition? I ask you, is that bullying and spiritual abuse? I tell you, it is.

I have seen what was done by community bullies, known as the IRA, over the years, and most recently to the poor policeman in Omagh in 2023, and I thought, 'that is what church bullies have done to many of us, injured us to such an extent that we will never work again in a church setting, or possibly elsewhere.' It has caused life changing damage to us. This has left us quite unrecognisable by many of our colleagues who quite easily walk by on the other side and do not even want to notice us. I have experienced that, and my friends in this position have experienced the same.

However, bad behaviour by ministers is unseemly, is it not? It is disgraceful, dishonourable, and indecent. And just as IRA terrorists have left DCI John

Caldwell beyond being able to work again, church bullies have done similarly to those they got their hands on. However, that is how the bully works, you see. He seems to know no other way of dealing with people, and even non-ordained employees of the church have found the same. They treated them like *scubala*; and that is a Greek word for dung, rubbish, excrement, (*Philippians* 3:8).

Without knowing it, Tim Field's list of qualities of a bully arrived at by research differs little from the opposite of that found in *1 Corinthians* 13. Nonetheless, power-greedy ministers do something else that opposes Paul's words. They *'rejoice in iniquity'* rather than *'rejoicing in the truth.'* You see, the minister's difficulties arose because he rejoiced in the truth, so much so that he preached the truth in his congregation. And that just was not acceptable to 'the people that count.' Moreover, every congregation has them, 'the people that count.' You know who they are. The moneyed people, the people of some social standing, etc. These are 'the people that count.' Into the bargain, they must be pleased at all costs. Not all elders of the church rejoice in the truth.

However, Gospel ministers do. So what do they do to them? They report them to the church courts, who then escalate the case to the highest court where the minister is being found guilty of some fabricated ecclesiastical misdemeanour. When that happens, to use the phrase, 'his goose is cooked.' He is 'dead meat.' Like the policeman in Omagh, he has been targeted for ages by these terrorist-like ministers. They made their preparations and now 'cooking time' has arrived. Clearly, we see human nature shining forth in all its ugliness in such situations. Is this bullying and spiritual abuse? I think you can see that it is. We think nothing of the media rejoicing in iniquity, in evil and wickedness of all kinds: but the church? We hear of the locker room talk and banter among men. However, you do not expect that amongst God's servants, do you? Worldly men will rejoice in iniquity and unrighteousness, but the church should be way above that, but is she? Locker room talk goes on among ministers of the Gospel, and it is not always wholesome.

How does this happen? Well, it can happen only when love is not the driver, the motivator, in all that they do. When they remove love from the situation, anything goes, and you think of the power surge they get when they succeed in destroying a brother minister, and they rejoice in that. They know they have the power! When they take love out of the equation, men can be economical with the truth, and, as one articulate politician put it, use 'terminological inexactitudes.' That also happens! Oh, how urgently the church must repent of her sin and her sins because her sin and her sins are of deepest dye. She must beg God for mercy so that He will wipe away her sins, and wash them away in the blood of Christ shed for them. She must prostrate herself before God's merciful throne and plead for forgiveness. She must return to the faith she has left ages ago.

Now it is only when she returns to the truth will she bear all things, believe all things, hope all things, v.7. Sadly, she bears with ministers who do not preach the Gospel, and they are there in the churches.

I just heard the other day of a minister who went to a funeral service in Northern Ireland and there was not even the mention of Jesus' Name in the officiating minister's message. No mention of sin or grace, nothing of that. Yet these men are protected by the church establishment. It just turns a blind eye to those who deny Christ by refusing to declare *the whole council of God.* They believe all the things their supporters tell them, but not those they are investigating. By default, targets are not to be believed!

What a travesty of the truth that is, and what a negation of *1 Corinthians* 13. How our Holy God must be appalled and grieved at what goes on in churches today. Is it any wonder we do not know the divine blessing, as we should? Is it any wonder that people are leaving the churches in their droves? It is no wonder that God has not poured out the Spirit upon us! Must we be surprised that the *'windows of Heaven'* have been closed against the prayers of God's saints? Should we wonder why the attendance at public worship is declining year on year? Church buildings are being closed faster now than at any time in the past. Ought we to be surprised at this turn of events?

We look at the Church of England legislating for what is utter depravity in that denomination. They are passing the most depraved laws, laws that are utterly offensive to the Holy God. However, other churches are not much different, are they? They pride themselves in their evangelical credentials, but they are no different. Evangelicals can be as nasty, unloving, and uncaring as the liberals. They, too, act sinfully against their brothers.

What must the church do? She must repent of her sins. She must listen to those who are hurting, whose hearts are breaking, and whose lives they have damaged, some of them beyond repair, and take urgent remedial action. She must see herself as God sees her. She must see herself as people who are completely undermining and denying what Paul is saying here in this chapter.

When she sees herself as God sees her, she will be broken before Him, beg for His mercy, beg for forgiveness, and beg God to be gracious to her once again. She will come and fall before the Cross of Christ, and cry out to God to be merciful. She dare not ask for judgment. None of us dare do that, but she must act. Ask for mercy.

Get that message out to your church. Let your minister know that they are in the wrong and that they have done wrongly against the Lord's servants. There is *sin in the camp*, and the church must identify and remove that sin. She must repent and seek God's forgiveness.

Prayer:

O Lord, our gracious and loving God, as we bow humbly before You, we come, Lord, before You once again, as those who are naked in Your sight. We can hide nothing from You, O God. You know our hearts. You know our secret thoughts. You know, O God, what the church has done, and what she is doing. You know that there is a hardness in our heart towards those who are vulnerable, weak, and needy.

Father, we pray that You will have compassion on Your church, on Your people, and grant that those Who are Yours may no longer continue to live, knowing that great wickedness has been done in their name.

So Father, deal with us in mercy and bring us back into fellowship with Yourself. We ask all these prayers in the Name of Christ Jesus our Lord. Amen.

11. The Fire *Still* Burns!

1 Corinthians 13:4-8a

Today is a very significant day for me. It is significant because 30 years ago on this very date, the church where I grew up, was ordained to the Christian ministry, and in which I served, the Presbyterian Church in Ireland, removed me from my congregations, leaving us practically homeless and without means of support. This was the fruit of months of bullying and spiritual abuse by my denomination.

Some months before this, while still in ministry and living in the manse, I had seriously contemplated suicide as the only way out of the pain that I felt, and 15 months after being discharged from my congregations, my mental health broke down, causing multiple problems ever since. My psychiatrist placed me under psychiatric care and was there for 18 long months and was on the verge of being sectioned or admitted to psychiatric hospital for my own safety on at least two occasions. Then followed three decades during which my usefulness in God's work was seriously impaired, though God, by His amazing grace, kept His hand on me and used me in His service.

As I reflect on this wicked behaviour by my denomination, I acknowledge the hurt and damage that it has caused to my family and me; but I also bear witness to the wonderful grace and mercy of God my Father during all these years. I give God all the glory for the fact that I am still here today and speaking to you. I give Him all the glory for the abysmal failure of my church to destroy me. I have been active for most of that time in Christian Ministry. He was and is my Defender, my Shield, my Hiding Place, my Strength, my Strong Tower, my Refuge. To God alone be all the glory.

The evil of bullying and spiritual abuse has continued unabated in the churches. While I have been the first in living memory, I have not been the last, sadly. Within the context of the Christian Church, 'bullying and spiritual abuse' is essentially a Gospel issue. Strip away all the fat, all the fancy talk, all the virtue signalling, and this 'holier-than-thou' attitude, and this is where it comes down. It is a Gospel issue. It is as basic as that! It is a very serious matter. In fact, 'bullying and spiritual abuse' is an outright denial of the Gospel of God's grace. It is a Gospel issue.

The reformer John Calvin in writing about the Gospel said this: *'The gospel is not a doctrine of the tongue, but of life. It cannot be grasped by reason and memory only. But it is fully understood when it possesses the whole soul, and penetrates to the inner recesses of the heart.'* How perceptive that is! The Gospel is not just something a man professes. Anybody could profess the Gospel. You could train a parrot to profess the Gospel.

Therefore, it is not just about a profession; it is about a life that is lived in accordance with the Gospel. And if the Gospel of grace is not seen there, then there is a very simple explanation for that. It is because grace is not in the life. Once the Gospel grips a man's life, it becomes visible and evident. Like a city that is set on a hill (*Matthew* 5:14), it cannot be hidden. Why is that important? For this reason. If the Gospel does not change a man's life, then it is not the Gospel of our Lord Jesus Christ, nor of the New Testament. What is more, in a life that has not been changed, there is one reason for that, and that is that his relationship with God has not been changed, and only the Gospel, working in tandem with the Holy Spirit, can do that. He is still in his sins. He has not been regenerated, nor has he been reconciled to God. He is living in his sins and if he does not repent, he will die in his sins, as Jesus warned the people of His day. That is how serious this whole matter is!

Bullying and spiritual abuse is a Gospel issue primarily. Once the Gospel grips the soul, bullying and spiritual abuse will become impossible in the church, in the individual, or anywhere else. The moment a sinner's relationship with God is transformed, evil behaviour becomes the most self-contradictory thing imaginable, and for which he will repent.

Now, we looked at the general qualities of the bully, but now I must try to define what I mean by bullying. That is important. We need to know what we are dealing with when we talk about an issue like this. So let me give you a definition, a description, of what bullying actually is. Bullying is 'persistent, offensive, abusive, intimidating, malicious, and insulting behaviour. This abuse of power makes the recipient feel upset, humiliated or vulnerable. It undermines his self-confidence and causes him to suffer stress.'

There is something else about it. Bullies often try to defend themselves by saying, 'but I never intended to hurt you. I never intended to insult you.' However, the experts define bullying largely by the *impact* of the behaviour on the individual, not its *intention*. The negative effect of this on the target makes it bullying.

Over the years, I have used three metaphors to describe bullying. These are *terrorism*, *abortion*, and *rape*. Each of these is horrible in the extreme. In this chapter, I will deal with the first two and then I will deal with the third in the next chapter. So as I try to explain these metaphors for bullying, let me personalise it for the sake of clarity. They apply in my case in several ways.

First of all, *terrorism*. I was being 'set up' for relentless attack by church elders and ministers with a view to my destruction. Set up. Does that not remind you of how terrorists work? Christian grace was not in evidence at any time through this torturous process. The Judicial Commission held secret meetings with my opponents to which I was not invited. They held these meetings without my knowledge to discuss what their strategy would be to remove me from my congregations. At that time, I did not know that this was going on, but I heard about it later. They wanted to make sure that they got rid of me and they wanted to do it legally as far as church law was concerned. I was in the sights of these scheming, ecclesiastical politicians-turned-terrorists. Their aim was to get rid of me; I was to be removed, or better, destroyed.

That was how one elder put it when asked by a church member where he was going all dressed up. 'I'm going to put that man (me) from ever preaching again.' There is only one way to stop a called minister from 'ever preaching again' and that is by killing him. So they targeted me for destruction.

You see, all terrorists are trained killers. They kill what stands in their way, and every perceived threat to them must be removed by whatever means. This they very nearly succeeded in doing when I contemplated suicide while still living in the manse. These churchman showed no concern whatever for my health and they did not care for my wife and family.

You remember the Bible says something about *'Love your neighbour.'* It teaches something about *'love one another.'* I did not see any of that. Christian love or Christian charity had long since 'fled the nest,' and there was now nothing left but brutal legalism. Grace had disappeared. They had to get rid of me by whatever legal means was at their disposal. And this is what they did, exactly that. It was brutal, as all terrorism is; and we saw that just the other week, in the attempted murder in Omagh, Co. Tyrone, of DCI John Caldwell.

Therefore, terrorism is a very powerful metaphor to describe bullying and spiritual abuse.

The other metaphor that I have used is the metaphor of *abortion.* I use this because that is what the church did to me. She aborted me from my congregations. Abortion is the action that medical professionals take to murder a living unborn baby while still in the safety of his mother's womb. It is a planned action, therefore, it is premeditated. They gain the consent of all the parties to the destruction of human life, except, of course, the consent of the child that is to be murdered. The instruments of death are at hand, and soon the life of the unborn baby is no more. The unborn baby is an inconvenience and/or an embarrassment. They destroy the child without mercy, just as the parents of baby Finlay destroyed their son's life.[5]

In my case, like any abortion, the church secured the consent of all the parties to this murderous act, and they worked together in unison. However, the one person in the equation whose consent was not secured, was mine. Just like the unborn baby to be murdered, no one asked me to give my consent to this operation to remove me. They did this 'cloak and dagger' style. Only those who refuse to face the facts can miss the parallels between these two actions.

In actual abortions, the little baby does all it can to avoid the forceps of death grabbing hold of it. It

---

[5] 10-month old baby, Finlay Boden, was murdered by his parents and died on Christmas Day, 2020.

wriggles about, trying to avoid being dismembered, limb by limb, from its little torso.

That describes my reaction to every attempt at ecclesiastical abortion. Every attempt these church abortionists made to destroy me, I tried, unsuccessfully, to avoid. I could see their forceps pulling me apart. I could feel them tearing me from the inside out. They damaged me seriously, but I survived their planned abortion of me.

Abortion in the church scenario is usually what happens to those in the church who become surplus to requirements, because the management no longer views them as useful or convenient to them. Maybe they see them as obstacles to their progress, to their career advancement. Through all kinds of machinations, my foetal existence was an embarrassment to the establishment, such an embarrassment that they did not wish to talk about them, except in hushed tones. They viewed me as a danger. I was likely to spread 'disease' in the entire body. I had to be aborted and dispensed with. In fact, when my former Presbytery installed a new minister, they told him to have nothing to do with me because I was 'a very dangerous man'! That is actually what happened.

When the church agrees on an abortion, it is a planned and professionally executed procedure. The church establishment had succeeded in its plan, and those involved could get on with their lives with much less discomfort, as they saw it.

The good thing about it was that though they aborted me from a religious organisation, they did not abort me from the Church of Christ. I was always, and I still am part of God's *ecclesia*, the 'called out' ones. I remained in the Body of Christ. I was able to continue with my ministry, albeit in a more limited way.

So, actually, I survived an attempted abortion by the Presbyterian Church in Ireland, a fact that brings no pleasure to their hearts, why? Because they saw that they failed. I am still actively involved in Christian ministry and I can now do it without the pressure of being preyed upon by those who are not big into the Gospel. Some of these men are loyal to the Gospel only so far as their comfort allows, & no further!

However, this left me with the deepest discomfort and pain imaginable, and also, my wife and two young boys. It was indescribable. The hurt they caused me was beyond calculation. The entire process left a deep stain on my life that would remain with me until I die.

Why am I telling you this? I am telling you this because bullying and spiritual abuse are brutal. It is excruciatingly painful ill-treatment. When the church targets the minister for this cruel treatment, it goes without saying that the church targets his wife and children at the same time. The bullies know that what they do to the minister, they do to the entire family.

I recall how the IRA operated in Northern Ireland. As someone who worked in a pastoral role with what they describe as 'the collateral damage' of their actions, I saw the irreparable damage they did to those families. When they targeted the father/husband, they, by default targeted the entire family, including siblings and parents and extended family members. When the IRA murdered my youngest brother, I saw my father age by about thirty years. He became a little old stooped man who was just in the prime of life.

This is one thing in the context of terrorist criminality, but it is an altogether other thing when this same action is taken against an entire family within a professing Christian church. Those who did such nasty things must own up and admit their evil actions, make full confession of their sins to the Lord, beg his mercy and forgiveness, and ask to be restored to His favour once more. They cannot go on ignoring it. Just because they ignore the facts does not make them go away. They are still facts.

However, there is forgiveness with the Lord, that He may be feared, (*Psalm* 130:4). I would encourage them, even though they did me great harm, to confess their sins, to admit to our gracious God what they had done; to return to the Lord with brokenness and with deepest sorrow, and seek His forgiveness and His mercy. If they read this chapter, I can only plead with them, out of a heart of love for them, to come back to the Lord and to receive His forgiveness once again.

Prayer.

O Lord, our gracious God and Father, with all the pain of this day, I come to You with thankfulness in my heart, for Your good hand being upon my wife and family for the last thirty years.

Thank You, Lord, for Your mercy. Thank You for Your grace, grace that was totally undeserved. Thank You for Your faithfulness to Your broken servant. Thank You, Lord, for keeping Your good hand upon me all these years. And thank You for using me in some little way in the service of the Gospel.

Today, we pray for those bullies and spiritual abusers within the churches. They are there, Lord, and You know they are there. Unitedly, we ask that You will come to them, that You will deliver them from this wickedness, from this sinfulness, and that they might seek You as never before, ere they stand before Your judgement Throne on that last day.

So Lord, be merciful to us all. Give us Your grace.

We ask all these things in Jesus' Name. Amen.

12. Church Rapists!

1 Corinthians 13:4-8a

Now, we saw last time that several metaphors may be used to describe bullying and spiritual abuse. These are *terrorism* and *abortion*. In this message, I want to deal with a third metaphor that more than adequately describes the true nature of bullying and spiritual abuse, and that is the metaphor of *rape*.

Why do I use such a horribly emotive term to describe bullying and spiritual abuse? For this reason. Bullying and spiritual abuse is a horrible, cruel, and barbaric way of removing an unwanted minister from his congregations. Churches use this surgical tool to remove a minister, and they do it almost at a whim. There have no problems about doing this. Those who would do that to a servant of Christ will have no problem about being ambivalent about abortion, or the murder of unborn babies. The two things go together very neatly.

In this context, what is the relationship of rape to bullying and spiritual abuse? Let us look at it and see what I am saying. The powerful and disturbing concept of *rape* floods my mind when I think about what the churches do to their ministers, mostly, if not exclusively, to evangelical men, with all the horrendous emotions associated with that kind of personal violence. Rape is essentially about the 'abuse of power,' just as bullying is, and only secondarily about intrusive sexual attack or violation. What the church did to me and to a growing number of other ministers was nothing less than barefaced rape.

Consequently, it is very easy to see that bullies and abusers share the same way of working, the same mind-set, the same ambition, and the same goal, as rapists. Now, this takes two distinct but related forms. *First*, there is the idea of *'date rape.'* I experienced several incidents of 'date rape' when Presbytery invited me to meetings, where it subjected me to strangling emotional abuse by men with a stake in getting rid of me.

This caused quite severe stomach nerves as the time for the meeting drew near. As well as the Presbytery Clerk asking me to violate my conscience over a certain issue, he told me that unless I did so (that is where the element of threat came in) the consequences would be terrible. One of those consequences was having my case referred to the powerful Judicial Commission of the Presbyterian Church in Ireland. This is the body that has 'the power of life or death over ministers,' especially Gospel ministers. This is not surprising given the anti-Gospel nature of a theologically liberal denomination. So the rape went on, meeting after insufferable meeting. That was *'date rape.'*

Allied to this was the second form that it takes. They also subjected me to episodes of *'gang rape,'* with key players 'doing the job' and the onlookers supporting and enjoying what they were witnessing, though some were silent and confused at first. This was excruciatingly painful. It was painful especially because these were colleagues with whom I was working at the time, some of whom I trusted. After that savage experience, and looking back with the benefit of 30 years' hindsight, I still find it difficult, if not impossible, to trust ministers, unless and until they prove to be good friends.

'Gang rape,' as you would imagine, involves the multiplying effect of rape by a single person, a single individual. When one finishes and gains his moments of pleasure, the others are lining up to gain personal gratification as they continue the psychological torture.

During and after such episodes of 'gang rape,' I was left emotionally exhausted and wondering why men in clerical collars were doing this to me! Had I committed such terrible ecclesiastical crime that warranted such abuse and pain? That was my question. Never before had I heard of the church giving such treatment to anyone.

I had always believed that there were but two reasons for which the church can remove a man from his ministry and these were serious theological error, or heresy, and/or immoral living. However, neither of these applied in my case. This left me deeply perplexed and exasperated. I had asked senior members of Presbytery questions to which I wanted answers, and I was relieved to hear that I had done nothing wrong. But I then asked them, 'What is the problem?' to which question I was not given any answer. If there was no problem, why were they subjecting me to this vile treatment? Why was I being threatened with what was essentially 'hanging' for a 'non-offense'? Only later did I realise that the Presbytery was working to a hidden agenda invented by the Judicial Commission to have me removed because of my involvement in the anti-ecumenical CCWRT group within PCI. I told them, 'If you refer my case to the Judicial Commission, I was finished, for that is the way to hell for every evangelical minister.' They disagreed. They did not believe that that was the case, saying it was only going for 'further investigation.' This really hurt me and left me utterly confused about what was happening to me, and why.

I have no doubt that some will treat this report as untrue. They will view it as exaggerated, embellished for effect, and 'egged up' in some way or other. Why will they react in that way to what I am saying? Here is the reason: the rapist and those who support him do not believe rape victims, nor do those to whom they report the crime. What you see in the public square is not what the reality is 'behind the counter.' There is no doubt that PCI has been infiltrated at every level, from top to bottom, by those who embrace the false religion of theological liberalism, the religion of unbelief. These infiltrators pose as evangelicals and with the result that they deceive the unwary.

Then, there were the bystanders who saw what was going on, but did absolutely nothing to stop it or to offer me any protection from my attackers, not one. These were experienced pastors. These were men who, on the surface, were looking after the spiritual well-being of their members, and here was I, a colleague, a servant of Christ and the Gospel, being hounded and battered and bruised and crushed by the church's establishment; yet not one of them raised a voice of dissent. They could have intervened were it not for fear of what Presbytery might do to them also, if they got on its wrong side and backed the man whom they wanted to remove. It is still true that 'turkeys don't vote for Christmas.'

The form of deception used was despicable. Boy, it hurt; and it still hurts. You know that when their case goes to the Judicial Commission, evangelical ministers are as good as 'dead meat.' It was a barefaced lie for them to tell me that it was just going for further investigation. I suppose that should not surprise me because bullies, just like alcoholics, are compulsive liars. I had to learn this the hard way and to my great cost.

I never expected this to go on in the Church, of all places. I had always thought that evangelicals believed the Bible to be the Word of God, all of it, and that it applied to every realm of life and living. But, boy, was I wrong in that? *1 Corinthians* 13:4-8a do not seem to have any place whatsoever in the thinking, in the faith, in the theology and practice of the ministers who dealt with my case.

When you speak about what the church did to you, you *become the problem* and *they* feel *they* have to *deal* with *you*. This is bizarre, utterly bizarre. I have seen this with a friend from another denomination who is speaking out loudly about what his church did to him, and now he is *the problem*. This is how the bullying and spiritual abuse dynamic works itself out.

The fact is that when victims of church bullying speak out about the problem, they are *not causing* the problem; they are simply *exposing* the problem. They are pulling back the carpet to see what the church has covered over for generations.

The problem of bullying and spiritual abuse is rife within the churches, but they do not want it to be exposed. Why? There are two reasons that I can think of. *First, because* bullying is essentially the work of the devil, he does not want *his work* exposed because *he* does not want to be exposed. He is much happier working from the shadows, and doing what he has to do through human flesh, through men, through ministers. *Secondly*, if this is exposed then they would have to do something about it. There would have to be fundamental change in the way the church operates. Church bullies might have to be exposed.

The third century AD church father, a man by the name of Cyprian, said, 'He cannot have God as his Father, who does not have the church as his mother.' There is truth in this, is there not? But, what are you to do when your mother is abusive? Are you to stay there until she damages you beyond repair? Do you go elsewhere? What is your response to be? When the church becomes an abusive mother to her children, then in my view, she ceases to be the Church of Jesus Christ. A former clerk of the General Assembly highlighted the indecent haste with which PCI mishandled my case, when he admitted at the next General Assembly in June 1993, that they had not given sufficient time to look at my case.

I have been reading a book by Dr Gardner Spring on the cross, entitled, *'The Attraction of the Cross.'* He writes concerning the trial of our Lord Jesus Christ. The leaders of the Jewish church conducted His trial 'with an outrage upon the very forms of justice and humanity.' And, you know, that sums it up in my case. He goes on to speak of Caiaphas, the high priest and president of the Sanhedrin, and he said that 'he seemed at once to prejudge the question.' PCI had its hour, when the power of darkness reigned. Writes Spring, when Jesus was being judged by the Sanhedrin, it was 'a night of fatigue and anguish for Him,' the Lord Jesus Christ, 'but to the Jewish church leaders it was chagrin and malignity.'

It would be wrong, it would be remiss, it would be inaccurate and untruthful of me to leave it there. I can bear testimony to the fact that I found God faithful through it all. He walked with me along this rugged road, where there were many ambushes, snares, and falls. However, like the distressed disciples in the boat on the Sea of Galilee, I, too, was comforted by the fact that the Lord Jesus Christ was with me through it all. He is our only Refuge in trouble.

I urge you who are reading these words, speaking directly to you, to flee to Him. Run to Him this very moment and stay with Him until the 'storm clouds lift' and the storm passes by; for it will. Whatever storm you may be passing through at this time, Jesus Christ is the only real Refuge that there is.

Moreover, when you are down, when others have kicked, bruised, and crushed you, it is to Christ alone, our Refuge and our Strength, that we can flee, in whom we can trust and in whom we can hide. He is faithful who promised. He is the covenant God after all, and as the covenant God, He not only makes promises, but I can testify to the fact that He also keeps the promises that He made.

Prayer:

O Lord, our gracious, blessed, and loving God, whatever life throws at us, we can turn to You. We can turn to You and trust You, and we can hide in You. We can see in You Someone who is utterly trustworthy. We can hide in You, O God, when the storms are raging around us, and maybe even in our own lives, and in our own hearts.

Lord, we ask that You will show us great mercy and grace. You have done it for me and You can do it for those who are going through this horrendous experience.

So Lord, as we commit ourselves now to You, we pray that Your almighty grace and strong arm will be put around us, and that You will bear us up and

*enable us to look in faith to the Lord Jesus Christ,
our risen, exalted, and reigning Lord and Saviour.
Amen.*

13. Defining the Victims/Targets of Bullying and Spiritual Abuse!

The victims of bullying and spiritual abuse did not cause the bullying, any more than victims of flooding or burglary caused natural disasters or crimes. The bullies cause the bullying. Victims become victims, they become something they were not before, and they are made victims because they were perceived to be easy targets. Bullying does psychological damage to the victim. Or, in other terms, it inflicts psychiatric injury on them. That is what bullying behaviour does, and it is becoming more apparent as further research is published on this issue that this is the result of it. Fear, self-doubt, impotence, rage, all surface in the experience of the victims of bullying and spiritual abuse. Perhaps the most pervasive impression that this makes is that of the victim's bewilderment, the sense of shock or trauma that this could possibly be happening to him. In most, if not all, cases of bullying, the problem resides solely with the bully, being without justification and making the life of the victim intolerable.

While there is some truth in that, I must admit, we must be very careful not to remove from the perpetrator the responsibility for his anti-social actions. To blame others, even partly, or to blame your experiences for such antisocial behaviour is to go too far in that direction. The big problem with Freud's position is that it has 'sanctified irresponsible behaviour and made it respectable.' There is much evidence for this in the world today.

That admitted, we cannot deny the influence of other people on our behaviour. The individual carries the responsibility for his own actions. We have looked in a recent study at some of the characteristics of the bully. Now I want us to look at the general qualities of the victim. As we do that, keep those four verses from *1 Corinthians* 13 open before you, for there you will see a remarkable similarity between them.

These general qualities were arrived at as a result of research done by Dr Tim Field, and among them are to be found the following, that the victims of bullying are generally kind, sharing, empathic, sensitive individuals. They are honest, trustworthy, and conscientious. They are reliable people, always thinking of others, good with people. They are people-focus, helpful, constructive, popular, committed to service. They are long-term thinkers, not short-term thinkers such as we have around us today. They are multi-focused, and they like to feel valued. They like to do a good job. They converse easily with others, are sociable, selfless people. Generally, you find that they are good-humoured and intuitive. They have a sense of injustice, they are charitable, have a strong sense of conscience, are conciliatory and modest.

Now, you might as well be reading the expansion of 1 *Corinthians* 13 when you read these general qualities that have been arrived at as a result of secular research. These are basic Christian virtues found within the meaning of *agape*, love. If every church comprised those targeted by the bullies and spiritual abusers within the church, then you would think you were in Glory. Church leaders seem to target only the most Christ-like people. That fact alone confirms that Targeting for *bullying* is never a random act! *Spiritual abuse* is not something that someone does to you by chance! It is deliberate, premeditated, carefully planned, calculated, and intentional, wicked behaviour!

However, because we are still in the flesh, we, too, have weaknesses that plague our lives. You know that and so do I. There are tendencies, as shown by the bullied person, which include the following, according again to Tim Field's work. They exhibit low assertiveness at times, can be indecisive, and are over-dependent. They often seek and need approval. They need to be valued. They are prone to feeling guilty, are respectful, and meek. They are tearful when hurt. They have an instinct to do themselves down. And they give long answers to short questions. They very often put others' needs first.

Now, if that is not a description of *agape* love in the New Testament sense, then I do not know what is. The view that emerges is as revealing as it is consistent. It brings much needed consolation to the victims as it displays personal factors that are recognised by them, thus showing them that their psychological makeup makes it relatively easy for the bully to pounce on them. And they do that because of what? Because of the psychiatric injury that has been caused to the victim. Their often-justified fear of being virtually unemployable haunts the timid heart. They fear that they might never work again. In addition, I have seen that too many times. Those thoughts also crossed my own mind in the early days. However, people today whom the church has bullied think the same.

We must recognise psychiatric injury for what it really is. It is *injury*; it is not *illness*, although the injury can lead to illness if it is not treated, and healed quickly.

And then Tim Field goes on to say in very encouraging and pastoral terms that are characteristic of people who have suffered breakdown[6] as result of stress caused by bullying is 'their irrepressible desire not only to regain their former strength and carry on with their lives, but to tackle the injustice which is the cause of their injury.'

That is precisely what I am about and have been for almost 30 years. Field goes on, *'This is hardly the profile of the average person with a mental health problem. It's also important to remember that whereas illness may improve with time, psychiatric injury, as with most injuries, gets better.'* He adds in even more encouraging terms, that after a period of recovery which may take a couple of years or more, *'many people who have experienced breakdown bounce back again to even higher levels of attainment. Although their subsequent achievements are less likely to be measured in terms of finance, grade, or career progression.'*

These words are important reassurances to those whose lives bullies at work have traumatised and by bullies and spiritual abusers within the visible church.

Bullying is very much like a war situation, is it not? It leaves people injured, sometimes permanently. They have life changing injuries. The issues involved rotate around 'lies and deceit.' These are the servants of war, of course, and are linked inseparably

---

[6] Field, 109-121.

to bullying. They are the oxygen that bullying breathes. While the 'abuse of power' is at the heart of bullying behaviour, deceit fills the head.

This is insightful and challenging, is it not? While we can make no safe case for bullying as an amoral reality, a strong case exists for its inherently immoral character. It breaks the Moral Law of the Judaeo-Christian religion, the Christian faith, for example, which nearly all accept as an excellent standard of morality. Bullying is essentially lawlessness. The apostle John tells us in *1 John* 3:4 that *'lawlessness is sin.'* It is sinful behaviour. However, it is not recognised or acknowledged as sinful behaviour, but as a management tool to get what you want. It exhibits an antinomianism that recognises no standards of common decency. The bullying organisation or individual is therefore set on a collision course with decency, honour, and justice. In fact, it is on a collision course with the Lord God Almighty. In addition, any attempts to expose, eliminate, or prevent bullying will be hindered and opposed by an arsenal of lies and deceit, and denial that it even happens.

During the war in Croatia in 1994, the Radio Times wrote the following. *'Truth is the first casualty of war. All they discover when they visit ... Croatia is that no one can be trusted, no one is at ease, and no one tells the truth.'*

That describes the war situation very well, does it not? It describes what bullies do to their victims. They engage in lies and deceit. Truth does not enter the equation. You cannot believe the word of the people who do the bullying! Like the poor alcoholic, they are compulsive liars. What a tragedy that is that ministers who bully within the Church of Jesus Christ cannot be believed *just because they are ministers*! The very thought that ordained ministers operate in lies and deceit when dealing with others is deplorable in the extreme. It is one of the strategies used by people of corrupt mind. Trust is undermined, and falsehood established in its place. 'Truth forever on the scaffold; wrong forever on the throne.'

The church can eliminate bullying behaviour only if people value truth and justice, and desire their happiness and the well-being of themselves and other people. Because bullying and spiritual abuse have not yet been eliminated by the churches, that raises the question as to the truthfulness of those ministers who bully, and of those who support them. My experience of my accusers and judges using lies and deceit, and these being believed and acted upon, traumatised me and eventually broke my health. It is therefore impossible for justice to be done, and *be seen to be done,* when no attempt is made to discover the truth of the allegations being made.

Further, the victims of both forms of violence - bullying and rape - end up by asking themselves, 'What did I do to bring this on myself?' In fact, in Northern Ireland, the Equal Opportunities Commission defines sexual harassment as, *'The perpetration of unwanted and uninvited sexual advances (in physical and verbal form) on an unwilling victim.'* Rape is one possible outcome of sexual harassment. It is *unwelcome, uninvited, unwanted,* and it necessitates the *unwilling* cooperation of the victim. The desire to dominate the victim for personal gratification is paramount in rape. It is also paramount in bullying.

The victims of bullying are wholly unwilling participants in this depraved behaviour, just like the victims of rape. The parallels between these two social evils are so strong that only the blind can miss them.

But there are differences, of course, one of them being that *'in bullying the victim is expected to find, arrest, charge, prosecute, and convict the offender, largely by his own efforts and whilst recovering from the experience, unaided, and using a legal system that is unsympathetic, uninformed, and often itself hostile.'*

So to the victims of bullying and spiritual abuse, I say to you, despite all that I have said before, take heart. Take heart, because you are not the evil person the bully has made you out to be, but someone who displays the essential qualities of an individual whose life is governed and driven by New Testament love, and those qualities are not evident in the bully's life. Do not give up. Do not do yourself down. Do not try to destroy yourself by negative thinking.

Christian brother or sister, get back to the Scriptures. Use the Scriptures as your supreme authority in these things. Compare what was done to you with *1 Corinthians* 13:4-8a. Indeed, compare what was done to you with the whole of *1 Corinthians* 13. You will see that you were on the right side. The bullies were on the wrong side of the truth. So take heart. You are *not* the bad person they made you out to be, nor are you the person who should be *cancelled* – and we know about the 'cancel culture' in our own society at this time. The church may have *cancelled* you out, and may have *ghosted* you. The church may even have deceived others concerning you. But remember this; as a child of God, as a servant of God, you are highly prized in His sight. He looks on you as *'the apple of His eye,'* as someone exceedingly precious, and you will have divine protection in your life.

Remember, there is a Day coming when these people of corrupt and depraved mind will have to stand before God the Judge, and give an account of the things done in the body, whether good or bad (*2 Corinthians* 5:10). As the victims of bullying, I must add, we also have to stand before the great Judge of the whole Earth. So let us humbly come before the Lord. Let us walk with him daily. Let us seek to exhibit these qualities of excellence that Paul lists for us, and let us live our lives with our eye on the future. What we see here in this life is not all that there is. There is coming a day when all wrongs will be righted at the Judgment Throne of God.

Prayer:

O Lord, we thank and praise You that we did not bring bullying or spiritual abuse on ourselves. We thank You, O God, that you have taught us that this was a decision made by others, men of depraved mind. We thank You, Lord, that You have cleared up this misapprehension in our own minds about this, that we were made something that we were not before, the victims of bullying and spiritual abuse.

Give us grace, O God, to live day by day, and to know that if we do not get justice in this life, real justice is coming, when truth will be vindicated, and all unrighteousness obliterated from Your very sight.

So, be with us, O God, and surround us by Your Spirit. May Your peace fill our hearts and may we walk in faith before You and before men.

This we pray in Jesus' Name. Amen.

14. Is Recovery Possible?

1 John 3:1—4, 10-18

As we draw this series of sermons on the vexed subject of bullying and spiritual abuse to a close, I think it wise to be as pastoral as possible in order to help those living through and with this evil, and its consequences. Is recovery possible for the victims of bullying and spiritual abuse? That is a very big question. Can someone come back from what was a near death experience to live a positive and useful life after bullying and spiritual abuse? Is this the best that I can expect in what I am going through now? In other words, is recovery possible?

Well, the answer is 'yes,' and we must never allow our minds to be taken over by the suggestions of the evil one who will tell us that this is as good as it gets.

Or that this is all that is going to be for you. In a very real sense, you will have to live with the hurt, the wounds, and the damage that the church has inflicted upon you. However, the devil will tell you that you will never get over that vile treatment. But he is a liar, and has been a liar from the beginning, the father of lies.

While I was working with the traumatised victims of terrorism, the government wanted me to refer victims of terrorism to its agents for treatment. I refused. And I refused for a very good reason. I got to know an expert, a consultant in trauma treatment, very well in those years. I asked him if I was right to do as I had done, and he said that it would not be right to send traumatised people to those associated with the people who caused the trauma in the first place, because that will re-traumatise them. It will set them back almost to the very beginning.

I have made the problem within the church as clear and plain to you as I can. This is a very serious problem in the church. I would be failing in my duty if I were to ignore the subject, as so many preachers do. The churches know how to bully but they do not know how to care for those they have bullied. They do not know even how to show brotherly love to those they have destroyed by their bullying and spiritual abuse. So many churches have ignored it.

However, ignoring it is not an option. Pretending that this does not exist, as one very senior churchman said to me, is not a solution. She must face the facts head on. And because bullying and spiritual abuse in and by the churches have caused the problem, they are not the people to resolve it. Can I repeat that? Because bullying and spiritual abuse in and by the churches caused the problem, they are not the people to resolve it, for the very reason that the trauma consultant explained to me.

Their unholy behaviour puts colossal pressure on the bullied individuals, and they must lift off that weight. But the churches will not, because they are not willing to do that. Further, the people that they have traumatised by their bullying no longer trust them. They have no confidence in them and they will not go to them.

I said in a previous chapter that this culture of bullying and spiritual abuse is a Gospel issue. It is a denial of the Gospel of grace and faith. It was also an ecclesiastical, or church, issue because those who perpetrate this evil against their brothers are presenting the church in a very bad light. It is a distortion of the Gospel message and of the Gospel life. It is a distortion of what the Biblical church is. It totally undermines the Gospel and undermines the Church that the Gospel created. It challenges the whole idea of sanctification. It makes the Word of God of no effect, as Jesus taught in *Mark* 7:13.

Now, I would be the last person to trivialise what Christ's servants have been put through by the churches. I must say this, however. A reasonable level of recovery is possible for you. Do you hear that? A reasonable level of recovery is possible for you. It will be incomplete because it has left damage, and scars, injuries and wounds that are indelible. In fact, you will take these hurts to your grave. Thankfully, you will be able to function with a surprising level of normality.

So is there a remedy for those who have had this bullying and spiritual abuse inflicted on them in and by the church. And if so, what is it? Well, yes, there is a remedy, and I want to offer some guidance to you by way of giving pointers, and they are no more than pointers, that you might find helpful in your healing and recovering journey.

Experts in the field have identified two responses to bullying, to which I want to add a third. The two main responses are to stay in the abusive church and *fight* for change and reform. Fight your corner and do not be defeated by anyone. That is one response, the *fight* response.

The other response identified by the experts is to leave and go to a 'better' church. In other words, the *flight* response. There is nothing better than a clean pair of heels; get yourself out of it as fast as you can.

But, there is a third that I want to add to these. It is a very common response, and it is this, to *freeze*. This is why the victims or targets of bullying and spiritual abuse are traumatised; they feel powerless to do anything about their situation. They ask the question, 'What are we to do? Where can we go? To whom can we turn?' And in that abusive situation, they feel

trapped. They feel and are numbed emotionally, unable to feel or act or make necessary decisions.

I remember when ministers with whom I have had very close relationships had died, my response away back at that time was to shrug my shoulders in a kind of 'so what' response. I experienced emotional numbness. Your denial of what ministers did to you, or freezing up, is the God-given ability to avoid emotional, spiritual, and psychological pain. That is how God made us! When the level of pain we experience becomes so intense, we numb it out emotionally. We went into denial mode, into avoidance mode. We will not admit that it happened. We will not admit what we have gone through; that we have been hurt, and injured and damaged by what the Church has done to us. And in your powerlessness, you just do not know what you could possibly do to help yourself.

Does that explain why ministers who are the victims of bullying and spiritual abuse no longer go to church at all? Some go either to a different denomination or to a non-denominational grouping. Is that why? They are stuck; they do not know what to do! And does not that explain why ministers' wives have no heart in going to church? And what about their children? So often they, in turn, turn against religion altogether as a direct result of what the church had done to their

father. The fallout of church bullying and abuse is much wider than the targeted minister. The entire immediate family is embroiled in it.

My aim now is to suggest some guidance to help you break out and get back into a healthy relationship with God and His church. Some ministers and members feel trapped in their abusive churches.

Let me explain to you the nature of these spiritual traps.[7] What is a good trap? The traps that the church has set for people like you and me have been so effective that they have trapped us. Thank God,

---

[7] Johnson, D, and VanVonderen, J. *The Subtle Power of Spiritual Abuse* (Minneapolis: Bethany House Publishers, 1991), 183ff.

He has delivered me from that. But at that time I was trapped. I could see no way out.

Well, *first*, a good and effective trap is one you can enter easily, like mice, but find that getting out of it is impossible. That is a good trap. Speaking to ministers today who are going through this awful experience would never even contemplate getting out of that trap. They feel that they cannot. Too much is dependent upon what the trappers offer to them. This reminds me of the Stockholm Syndrome.

Secondly, a good trap must have attractive bait to lure you into it. You know that is the case. In the ministry, you have a life-long job so long as you do what your people want you to do. You have a free house, and good expenses. You have a life-long job with a good salary and pension. Who would want to give that up? Surely, it is better to put your head down, do what the institution, the *politburo*, wants you to do, and forget about your principles, forget about your conscience, forget about your ordination vows. That is the second trap. It is so powerful, so appealing, so comfortable.

A statement that a CIA officer made to a colleague in the James Bond film, *Quantum of Solace*, illustrates this perfectly. He said, '*I need to know you are in the team, Felix. I need to know you value your career.'* A perfect trap that many Gospel ministers can recognise easily!

The *third* trap is this; the more the prey struggles to get out, a good trap will leave them tired and more exhausted, because they can find no way out. What happens is that their struggling to get out of a good trap zaps you of energy, and leaves you bewildered into the bargain.

Fourth, a good trap must have a good fit between the trap and the prey. Let me illustrate that for you. You would not use a rat-trap to catch a fish! You use a trap that is appropriate to the people that you want to enslave.

Now it is clear that a spiritually abusive system is a

good trap. Leaders like power and they demand full obedience from those under their control. However, the *power to abuse others was not given to them!* They have taken that to themselves. They have abused the power that they have by virtue of their office within the church, the office of eldership. They instil into your subconscious mind that to disobey them is the same as disobeying God. And they use the term, *'submit to the courts of the church,'* but they very conveniently leave out or de-emphasize the essential limitation to this submission demand when they pass over, while repeating these very words, *'in the Lord'.* Submission in God's church must be *'in the Lord;'* in other words, it must be a submission in accordance with what the Lord says in His Word. If it departs from that, then you are under no obligation to submit to any court or any authority within the Church of Jesus Christ. These men are very clever, but the discerning see through their *cleverness* with ease.

So effective was this brainwashing in my case, that for years I believed that because my church rejected me, so did God. I believed this for a long time. Just imagine the emotional and spiritual stress under which this put me!

However, when a 'light bulb moment' came, when I understood that this was not true at all, well, I rejoiced in that! What relief, what deliverance, what liberation that gave me. Like the Psalmist, *'When I entered the sanctuary of God, <u>then</u> I understood their end,'* (*Psalm* 73:17-19). Only three verses! But they changed everything for me. Looking forward to the judgement day, the Psalmist could see that God had set these people in *'slippery places,'* and destruction is ahead for them. It could happen in a moment, and terrors will utterly consume them. Not a great prospect for the bullies and spiritual abusers, is it? That is what the Word of God says.

The abused brother can comfort himself with these words. What is happening to them is not the whole story, of course. The end has yet to come. God will administer justice fairly on that last Day. You can be sure of that. Judgement will square with the facts.

So, we can now live in the light of that Day coming. It is coming and we can comfort ourselves with God's truth. You see, Paul tells us that false prophets disguise themselves as servants of righteousness (*2 Corinthians* 11:13-15). Everything is great at the beginning, is it not? However, they make subtle changes that you do not even notice. Just like the frog: you put a frog into boiling water and it will jump out immediately. But put it into cold water and heat the water up gradually, that frog will stay there until it is boiled alive. That is how subtle this whole thing is.

Abusive churches work in this very way. The

enslavement that they bring upon ministers and members is a gradual process. It gets to the point where rather than comparing where you now are with the norm, you compare it with the last adjustment, the last encroachment on your liberty as a servant of Christ. You will not see much change; but when you compare it with the NT norm, you will see how far you have moved away and you find yourself now in this abnormal situation, this situation of entrapment.

Let me give you an illustration that might be helpful. Say, for instance, that the normal temperature is 20°C, and you are used to 20°C. Then the temperature rises to 22°C and again you get used to 22°C. Then it rises to 24°C, then 26°C, and then 28°C, and then 30°C, and you start to feel a bit hot at 30°C.

Now, if you compare where you are with the last change in temperature, you will see that it was only two degrees higher. I can live with that, you conclude. But, if you go back to the norm, if you go back to 20°C and compare the 30°C with the 20°C, you will see that there is a 10°C rise in the temperature.

That is what the churches do, all of them. They gradually entrap their ministers, insisting that they do what the presbytery, or the bishop, or the president, demands of them. They have no way of objecting to any of that. It is a gradual wearing down of the ministers and the people. If you are a church member, and you said, 'Well look, I would find it impossible to leave my church.' What are you saying? You are saying that you are in a spiritual or religious trap. If a minister says, 'Well, I could not possibly leave my church, my denomination.' What is he saying? He is admitting that he has been caught in a spiritual trap, and he neither wants to get out of it, nor can he see a way out.

But the good news is this. You do not have to stay there. You can break free from these clever traps that these clever people have brought into your pathway. How?

Well, let me give you four things to consider. Think about these in the presence of God as you mull over what I have been saying to you in these chapters. *First*, you must reach the point where you realize and admit to yourself and to others that the church has bullied and spiritually abused you, and seek help. That will be the first sign of liberation coming to you. No one will go to their GP unless they feel sick or ill, or they are worried about themselves. The same applies to a minister or a member of any church. Seek out someone who can help you. You are not on your own. There is help out there for you.

Secondly, you need to renew your mind, (*Romans* 12:1-2). Truly, you have been spiritually brainwashed by your bullies and by their loyal supporters. You have been deceived. You probably do not believe that or want to admit that you have been deceived. But *you have been deceived*. Religion is very seductive and addictive, and church religion is especially so. If you find yourself there, this is a clear sign of abuse; and the church must give victims the right information and the permission to call out what she has done to them, as bullying and spiritual abuse.

The only remedy for spiritual brainwashing is to be soaked in the truth of God's Word. Why do I say that? Because truth frees. Truth delivers. Truth liberates. Jesus said, you remember, *'You shall know the truth, and the truth will set you free,'* (*John* 8:32). Is not that what you want most of all today? To be free from that abuse, this is what you must do. Get back to Scripture. Get back to what the Word of God says that He can do.

Thirdly, you must find safe relationships where you can heal from your wounds, the wounds that the church has inflicted on you. You need to go to a safe place and to be with safe people, people who understand and empathise and will support you, without judging you. These people have been where you now are, and they can give you pointers as to the way forward. I can tell you from personal experience, this works.

Fourthly, you must come to see your true identity in

Christ. The bullying churches want to rob you of your identity in Christ. They do not want you to see yourself as a man or a woman *in Christ*. You have forgotten this in your struggle to survive an attempted abortion by the church, leaving your mind in turmoil.   The fact that you are a child of God is a gift of divine grace, a gift from God to you.   Realise that, and rejoice in that.

They want to take that gift from you, but do not allow them.   You are a child of God.   You have been converted to Christ.   The Holy Spirit has regenerated you.   You have been justified.   You have been reconciled to the living God.   What they wanted to do was to turn you against your best Friend, the Lord Jesus Christ.

Now, I say to you humbly, think on these things.   You can do these things.   They are worth a try.   You have nothing to lose by giving this a go, and you have everything to gain.   God will be with you in this.   He wants your recovery.   He wants you to know His smile on your life again.   He wants to use you again in His service.   God is not like the church and the church is not like God.   He is gracious and forgives; God restores, and God has promised *'never to leave you, nor forsake you.'*   *'As I was with Moses,'* He said to Joshua, *'so shall I be with you.'*   Rest on that! That is the absolute truth.

Prayer:

Thank You, Lord, for this heartening message that has come to us from Your Word.   Thank you, Lord, for your grace. We thank You that Your grace is extended every single day. We thank you that it is sovereign grace. Thank you, Lord, that it is always sent to the undeserving, to those who deserve the very opposite.

So Father, flood our hearts and our minds with Your grace, and help us to soak ourselves in Your Word. Help us to take the whole sweep of Your Word, and to use it, and to see that as the foundation for our faith, for our lives. Let us never listen to the wicked suggestions of the evil one, the devil, the slanderer of the brethren, who says to us that because the church has rejected us, so has God.

Father, help us to see our rejection by theologically liberal or extremist churches as a badge of greatest honour and help us to wear that badge with proper spiritual pride.

We ask all these things in Jesus' Name. Amen.

15. A Way Forward!

Concluding this series of sermons, I was gratified to read from a Facebook friend the following words. *'I also understand that ecclesiastical leaders have abused their congregants at times. That is sad and ought to be exposed and dealt with appropriately.'* I agree entirely with those words.

However, victims must know *what they* can *do* to aid their recovery. You can do this but it is not easy. Why do I say that? Because in spiritually abusive systems, wounds are added to wounds. The more wounds the bully can inflict, the more damage he does to his victims. They believe lies and they strengthen their defences. Bullying and spiritual abuse depend on lies and deceit. So the only antidote to these evils is truth. To recover from such treatment, victims must hear the truth. They need to understand the choices that are before them by the renewal of their minds, as Paul tells us in *Romans* 12:1,2.

It is also the case that to aid the recovery of the victims, those who caused it must be gracious enough to admit that what they did was wrong. They must take immediate steps to repair the personal and professional damage that they or their representatives did to you.   Very often, *justice delayed is justice*

denied. I say, 'very often,' for we must always leave room for the mysterious providence of our good God and Father!

It is true that bullying and spiritual abuse make victims extremely self-focused rather than Christ-focused. They strive to ensure that they do the right things, not to please the Lord Jesus Christ, but to please the people who are in authority in the church, and who hold their future in their hands.   They become preoccupied with keeping all the rules of the church in a bid not to draw unwanted attention to themselves.

However, what this does is this: it draws you further and further away from Christ and His Word.   You become preoccupied with yourself, with your own situation, with your feelings and emotions.   You are preoccupied with the fact that you cannot understand what is going on.   You have forgotten about Christ! He is *missed in the mist.*

Who is He? He is *'the truth,'* and as He said to us, *'the truth will set you free.'*   Setting forth the truth to us is what I have tried to do in these sermons.

Now, where does recovery begin? It begins with a renewed focus on God, on His sovereignty, on His holiness, on His righteousness, and on the fact that *God* is the Judge, not man. We start, as always, with God. We follow the example of Moses in *Genesis* 1:1, *'In the beginning, God...'* We fix our minds and our hearts on the God of the Bible.

How does recovery continue? It continues with keeping our focus on God and His Word. There is no other effective help for the Christian, really. Yes, men can do a lot. Thank God for those men who can understand the workings of the mind and the emotions; they have brought great help to their fellow human beings down through the decades. Ultimately, it is keeping our focus on God and His Word; that is how we recover. Going to those who caused the psychological trauma is not a good thing to do. They have their role in mitigating the pain and damage caused to us, but they cannot give us the recovery we so desperately need.

The bully's ultimate purpose, you see, is to take you away from your best Friend, the Lord Jesus Christ. That is his goal. He wants to do what he can to separate you from the Lord Jesus Christ. He wants to rob you of your salvation if he can – an impossibility if ever there was one. He wants to put you at odds with the Saviour. It really is very nasty work, is it not?

What the devil does not want you to do is to come back to Christ. He wants you to stay away from Him. For it is to return to the Christ of the Scriptures, and to rest on Him alone, and to soak yourself in His Word, to learn to love Him all over again, and to make a fresh surrender of yourself to the Lord Jesus Christ, that recovery begins and continues.

That is what the devil and his minions do not want you to do! So, to escape that, to rise above that, you have got to take the decision to come and re-focus your life on the Lord Jesus Christ and on the Word that He has given. The church has bullied people almost to the point of death and some of us were very close to that. A Christian friend encouraged us not to become bitter at the perpetrators, but to hand them over to God, the perfect Judge; *for vengeance is Mine. I will repay.*' And He did! The churches are almost now at closing point, and they have a part-time minister. *'God's wheels grind slow, but they grind exceeding small.'* How true that old proverb is!

Now, to recover, we must immerse ourselves in Scripture, and the one thing the Scripture will tell us is this; it will tell us who we are. The bullies have tried to take that from us, you see, but Scripture reinforces that repeatedly.

Who are you? Ask yourself that question; who am I? The answer is, 'You are Christ's. You belong to Him. You are God's child first and foremost, and God's servant by calling. You are a Prince and a member of the Royal family. You belong to the Royal household, the only Royal household that counts. The King of kings is your Father; the Lord over all lords is your Father.' Do you realize that this is true of you? Do you realize that the Creator of the universe is your Abba? That is your privileged position, and what a privilege it is! You are no ordinary person. You belong to the sovereign King; you are in Christ - just think about that. You are united with the Lord Jesus Christ, and that happened the moment you put your trust in Him. You are under His mighty protection.

Yes, the church has done bad things to you. But look at what God's enemies did to His only begotten Son! They crucified Him after abusing Him physically, mentally, and spiritually. *'God did not spare His only Son, but delivered Him up for us all. How shall He not with Him also freely give us all things?'* as *Romans* 8:32 tells us. God gave Christ for you. He became yours by sheer grace through faith in Him alone. You are now *in Christ*. Never forget that. He sees you as *'the apple of His eye.'*

Look, Jesus calls you to come to Him, *Matthew 11:28. 'Come to Me, all you who are weary and laden, and I will ease you.'* Now, that is a lovely translation from the Geneva Bible. *I will ease you!* I will ease you in your situation. That is what you want and need above all else, is it not? Ease? Relief? Then, you know where you can find it - in the Lord Jesus Christ only.

The call is to come to the Lord Jesus Christ. In the

earlier part of that chapter, we heard about the judgement of God. The *'woe'* of God. Here we hear the wonderful invitation of Christ for you to come to Him. And what does He do? He *eases* your burdens. He carries your loads, He will strengthen you, and He gives grace for the road. *'Take my yoke upon you and learn of me. I am gentle and lowly in heart. You shall find rest for your souls.'* Cast off that heavy yoke that worldly people have put on you. You cannot carry it. You have tried now for years, but it is getting you down, it has broken you. That is too much for you. But Christ's yoke is different. It is a good yoke. It is an easy yoke. It fits well on your shoulders.

But here is an alternative for carrying that burden for you. Learn of Christ. It is bringing us back again to focusing on Him. *'Take My yoke upon you, and learn of Me.'* *Learn* how He put it on there in

Gethsemane. He was broken, and in agony. See Him there as He sweat great drops of blood. What did He do? He said, *'Not My will, but Yours be done.'* In other words, He handed the entire matter over to God His Father.

That is the only thing we can do. It will not stop our suffering, mind you, but the burden will be less to carry. Sometimes we say to ourselves, 'Well, I've had enough of this. This is getting on top of me and I can't go on.' But when you hand it over to God, He assures you, *'Vengeance is mine. I will repay, says the Lord.'* He keeps His promise. Stay close to Him. God will act in His own time and way.

Remember that the day of vengeance is coming, and that is the Judgement Day, when God will deal with those who have tried to destroy you. Hand it over to Him. *'Not My will, but Yours be done.'* In *Matthew* 11:30, He tells us why His burden is easy? It is because He helps us shoulder the load. He is there with us. He has told us He *'would never leave us, nor forsake us,'* and, *'Though I am with you always, even to the end of the world.'* *'As I was with Moses,'* God told young Joshua, *'so I will be with you.'* And he did not have an easy time, either!

Brothers and sisters, why are we not taking these mighty promises of God seriously? You know them. I have repeated some of them to you. You probably

175

prayed them. But when hardy comes to hardy, you do not take them seriously. I was there, too. I went through that; I am not speaking down to you or being critical of you. I was there for years. I can give no reason why I did not take God's promises seriously, or why I no longer believed them. I have asked myself that question and I am asking you the same question. Why have you not taken these promises seriously? Why do you no longer believe them? Why do you think that they do not apply to you?

God spoke them, so they are for us, His children. If I

was to give you a promise, you might have reason not to believe it. But these promises are coming from the very lips of your Father in Heaven. You can come to Him as a child comes to his father. 'But Father, you said. Father, you promised.' He is the covenant God! He is the God *who cannot lie.'* That is who is speaking here, the ever-faithful One, the One who keeps the promises that He made.

You can depend on Him. He brought us through many dark days, with not a former colleague to even ask how we were doing, or where we even surviving! No, the church does not come alongside and give us the needed support.

But God was there always when we needed Him most. He was there! At times, we did not recognise

His presence, but He was there. We heard that *'still small voice'* of calm speaking into our hearts. It was as if Jesus said to us what He said to His troubled disciples on the Sea of Galilee. *'Do not be afraid; it is I.'* It is almost as if we heard Him saying to us, *'It's all right, I'm here now.'* Oh, the reassurance that brings to us! He drew near to us in mighty grace and loving mercy.

Finally, remember this. *Romans* 8:28 gives us monumental assurance when Paul writes, *'But we know that all things work together for good to those who love God and are called according to His purpose.'* Is that not utterly amazing? Paul is speaking from bitter experience here; he has been through the mill as well, far more maybe than you have been through. Look what he endured for the sake of the Gospel. We are in exactly the same boat, suffering for the sake of the Gospel, and yet he said this; *'all things work together for good,'* because God is sovereign, God is in this situation. Everything that has happened to you and to me, including the bad things, are part and parcel of the great eternal purpose of the living God. They all *'work together for good to those who love God.'*

O, make sure that you love God with your whole heart, and that you know that God has called you. Keep your love for God burning brightly. That is how you know He loves you. Love Him with your whole heart. He has done no wrong to you. God has not harmed you, hurt you, or distressed you. But men have! He has tested you; but what He put you through was non-destructive testing. This stands in clear distinction to what the bullies did to you when they tried to destroy you. He tested you to prove your worth.

So, I say to you, love Him, and go on loving Him. Have you been called by Him, according to His purpose, to be united with Christ and brought into fellowship with Himself? Are you one of the 'called of the Lord'? You are. That is why you are a Christian. That is why you are serving Christ. You are one of His. You belong to Jesus, children of the Lord. You are His.

Yes, I did go through all that, just as I am trying to explain to you today. And, yes, the devil will attack you as he attacked me, and he will hit you hard. But he does this as a defeated enemy of Christ. He knows his time is short, so do not worry about his evil attacks. They are bound to come. However, that proves 'whose you are and whom you serve.' Listen again. You are Christ's blood-bought children, and you will be where He is now, reigning in Heaven above with all *the saints who from their labours rest,'* and who have gone before you. That is our great hope, brothers and sisters. The bullies tried to take this hope away from us, and they have failed miserably. You and I are secure in the hand of God, and we can say a hearty 'amen' to that!

Prayer:

Lord, our gracious and loving God, we come to you in the triumphant Name of our Lord Jesus Christ. Thank you for bringing these great truths to our remembrance. Thank you, Lord, for refocusing our minds on those truths that will never fail. That we belong to Jesus. That we are Yours. Yes, that we are men and women in Christ. We have been called according to Your purpose.

Lord, help us to love You with our whole hearts. Help us to stay close to You, especially when the dark clouds hover over us, and when our minds and our hearts seem to be somewhere else, and darkness and blackness surround us. Help us, O God, to look to You and to cry out to You for mercy. And help us to know Your peace in our hearts; through Jesus Christ our Lord, we pray. Amen.

Printed in Great Britain
by Amazon